THOMAS BECKET
OF CANTERBURY

The Murder

FitzUrse, identified by the bear on his shield, is striking the cap from the martyr's head, while another knight (Tracy) wounds the cross-bearer, Grim of Cambridge, in the arm. Since the picture was painted *c.* 1190 the artist might have seen all these people in the flesh. He has resisted the temptation, to which most artists succumbed, to show Thomas as saying Mass at the altar on the right

THOMAS BECKET
OF
CANTERBURY

ALFRED DUGGAN

FABER AND FABER LIMITED
24 Russell Square
London

First published in mcmlii
by Faber and Faber Limited
24 Russell Square London WC1
Second edition mcmlxvii
Printed in Great Britain by
Latimer Trend & Co Ltd Whitstable

CONTENTS

7

NOTE TO SECOND EDITION

This edition incorporates amendments based on notes left by Alfred Duggan. These notes were the result of comments and suggestions made by Dr. David Knowles, O.S.B., and Dr. Helen Cam, C.B.E., whose help is gratefully acknowledged.

ILLUSTRATIONS

THE MURDER. BM Harl: 1502 *frontispiece*

FitzUrse, identified by the bear on his shield, is striking the cap from the martyr's head, while another knight (Tracy) wounds the cross-bearer, Grim of Cambridge, in the arm. The costumes are accurate, and since the picture was painted *c.* 1190 the artist might have seen all these people in the flesh, only twenty years before. He has resisted the temptation, to which most artists succumbed, to show Thomas as saying Mass at the altar on the right.

KING HENRY II *facing page* 81

From his first Great Seal, in use 1155-8. This is the Seal that Thomas used as Chancellor. The King must have approved the design, and it probably is reasonably accurate, for a mediaeval portrait.

THOMAS PARTING FROM POPE ALEXANDER *facing page* 144

From a French poem of about 1240, and therefore the costumes are not contemporary. But note that Pope and Archbishop ride like knights, their horses properly up to the bit; while the cross-bearer rides very pompously, and the Cardinals on the left sit like sacks. In the middle ages great men lived in the saddle, and most interviews took place on horseback.

ILLUSTRATIONS

ST. THOMAS OF CANTERBURY:
ARCHBISHOP AND MARTYR *facing page* 161

From a mosaic in the church of Monreale in Sicily. Joan daughter of King Henry II married King William of Sicily in 1177, and this mosaic was designed *c.* 1190. Therefore it was meant to be seen by people who had known Thomas when he was alive, and is probably the best portrait that has come down to us.

CHAPTER ONE

CHRISTENDOM

There was a merchant of Rouen named Gilbert, and to distinguish him from all the other Gilberts (for the Normans had no surnames, and only a very small selection of Christian names) he was also known as Becket, the man from the little brook; presumably the little brook flowed through the village of Thierceville in Normandy, where he spent his childhood. In early life he left Rouen to settle in the thriving town of London, the richest town in the far-spread dominions of the Norman race. We do not know what trade he followed, but he was successful, and presently lived on the rents of the house-property he had bought with his gains; that was more dignified than buying and selling, for a dealer is always tempted to cheat; as for investing money in business, that would be putting it at usury, which was not only a sin but a revolting manner of life, repugnant to all men of honour. If you did not fight, or work with your hands, the only honourable way of living in those days was by the ownership of land. To this Gilbert Becket on the 21st of December 1118 was born a son; he must have been a sickly infant, for the same day he was baptized in the parish church of St. Mary Colechurch, in Cheapside in London. It was the feast of St. Thomas the Apostle, so the child was named Thomas, a rather unusual name for a Norman.

But at this point fitzStephen, the most interesting of Becket's early biographers, breaks off to describe to his readers the glories of London, and we may as well do the same; though it is not the London of 1118 which must be described, but the whole splendid bustling world of twelfth-century Christendom.

It was a united world, almost without national boundaries. From Norway to Sicily, from Poland to Portugal, a common religion, a common way of life, a common system of education, a common language, bound together every literate man, from the vicar of the poorest chapel to the learned theologian lecturing in one of the cathedral schools. An author who wished to be widely read must write in Latin, for the local dialects of the peasantry varied from village to village, and a Saxon of Hampshire could hardly understand an Angle from York. But a man whose native tongue was French or Provençal, Italian, Spanish or Portuguese, could understand spoken Latin, though if he was an uneducated warrior he could not speak it himself. These modern languages had no established system of spelling, and in the twelfth century about the only books written in French were poems which the composer jotted down to help his own memory, and which only he could read when it was time to recite them aloud.

A clerk who knew Latin was competent to fill a post anywhere in the Latin world. In 1143 Robert of Chester was appointed archdeacon of Pamplona in Spain, with a commission from the Abbot of Cluny in Burgundy to translate the Koran into Latin for the use of Christian missionaries in the Holy Land. Alan of Tewkesbury was first a monk of Christ Church, Canterbury, then a canon of Benevento in southern Italy, then Prior of Canterbury, then Abbot of Tewkesbury. Thomas Brown began as chaplain to King Roger of Sicily, and ended as almoner to King Henry of England. But the connection between the Norman states of England and Sicily was very close. At one time in the twelfth century the Archbishop of Messina, the Archbishop of Palermo, the Chancellor of Sicily, and the Bishop of Girgenti were all Normans of English birth. Sometimes English clerks complained that too many English benefices were given to Italians, but the traffic was not entirely in one direction.

At the head of this international society were two international figures, and the great question that agitated twelfth century politics was whether these two figures were equal, or whether one was superior to the other. Everyone agreed that the Pope was the head of the Christian Church, in England as everywhere else. *Ecclesia Anglicana*, the English Church, was a new phrase which up-to-date Latinists thought more elegant than some longer expression, such as the Church among the English; but strictly speaking there was no such thing. There was the Province of Canterbury, with thirteen bishops under the Archbishop of Canterbury; and the Province of York, with two bishops under the Archbishop of York (though throughout this period Carlisle remained vacant, and only Durham obeyed York). There was no superior who could give orders to both archbishops except the Pope.

There was no doubt that the Pope was supreme over every clerk. His rival, the Emperor, claimed to be supreme over the temporal affairs of Christendom; but that claim was by no means so freely admitted. The Holy Roman Emperor was certainly the heir of Otto the Great, more dubiously the heir of Charlemagne, hardly by any stretch of the imagination to be considered the heir of Justinian and Constantine, though his supporters said so at the top of their voices when they felt excited. No one could become Emperor until he had been crowned by the Pope; that was agreed. But did the election of a new Pope need the consent of the Emperor? Guelfs (Papalists) and Ghibellines (Imperialists) fought over that question for hundreds of years. We know how the struggle ended; there is still a Pope and there is no Emperor. But in the twelfth century the issue was undecided, and most students of form would have backed the Emperor to win. For there was a weakness in the Pope's position; the procedure for his election laid down that ideally the Cardinals should be unanimous; but if unfortunately they were not then the candidate chosen by 'the larger and wiser' party should be enthroned. That was asking for trouble. There might occasionally be doubt as to which was the larger party, since some clerks claimed to be Cardinals while their right to vote was disputed by others; but obviously both parties thought themselves the wiser. So after most vacancies in the Holy See there was a Pope, recognized by those parts of Christendom which were out of reach of the Imperial Sword, and an Antipope, recognized by the Emperor and his adherents. This situation had already arisen when William the Conqueror became King of England, and one of the most important of the royal prerogatives was the choice between two claimants to the Triple Tiara; if a Bishop anticipated this choice, by sending in his submission before the King had made up his mind, that was a very serious form of treason.

Since the struggle between Thomas Archbishop of

Canterbury and Henry II King of England was fought out on an international stage, with both sides appealing continuously to the public opinion of international Christendom, it would be as well to describe the resources and prestige of the various foreign powers. First came the Pope, with the right to excommunicate any Christian, a right admitted by every subject of King Henry; but always pressed for money, frequently in exile, and, as Marshal Stalin pointed out in 1944, with no troops at his disposal. Second in English eyes, though Germans might put him first, came the Emperor; he ruled Holland, eastern Belgium, Germany, Switzerland, Italy north of Rome, and much of what is now eastern France; the rulers of Denmark, Bohemia and Poland were his vassals. He should have been the most powerful prince in the world, but there were nearly always several rebellions raging in different parts of his vast dominions, and his enormous army was usually needed in two places at once. He had great prestige, especially in social affairs; the titles he bestowed were much sought after, and any King was proud to marry his daughter into the Imperial family. But actually he had very little power to help or harm the King of England. He was too busy at home.

Third came the King of France, the Emperor's only rival as the heir of Charlemagne. His territory was bounded on tne east by the Meuse, Saone and Rhone, and the Count of Flanders paid homage to him, otherwise his dominions were much the same as modern France. At his coronation in Rheims he might collect the great Peers who were his vassals and boast himself a mighty King; but in fact his Peers seldom obeyed his orders, and frequently made war on him. The only district he actually ruled was the Ile de France, a small territory round Paris. He never forgot that the Franks in the old days had rescued Rome from the Lombards, and was a faithful son of the Church; naturally, since the Pope's enemy, the Emperor, was normally his enemy also. He was a greater authority on questions of chivalry than even the Emperor, for chivalry was a French invention, and French knights were admitted to be the most gallant and honourable warriors in the world.

The King of England would probably come fourth. England was rather a backwater, only civilized in the last century; but William the Conqueror had started with a clean slate, he had no Peers to bother him, and he ruled his remote island more absolutely than any other monarch in Christendom. But England only gave the King his royal title; Henry II was also Duke of Normandy, which obeyed him, and Duke of Aquitaine and Count of Anjou, districts which had to be coaxed rather than commanded. In military power he was probably stronger than the King of France, but once in his life he had to do homage to the King of France for Normandy, Aquitaine and Anjou, and to his contemporaries that made him inferior.

The King of Scotland did homage to the King of England, though whether that was for his Kingdom or for his English Earldom of Huntingdon was a legitimate matter for argument. He might help the King of England in his French wars, but rather as an independent ally than as a vassal. England had not yet made a serious attempt to conquer Scotland; the few wars between the two countries had been caused rather by Scottish raids to the south, and relations were usually friendly. Probably the King of Scotland would be reasonably loyal so long as the King of England respected his dignity and refrained from giving him orders in public.

Ireland was in its normal condition of anarchy. There was a High King, but none of the lesser kings obeyed him. The Irish paid no tithes, and their Bishops were subject to the Abbots of the great tribal monasteries. This was regarded as very disgusting, and any decent Christian who had the leisure should conquer the country and teach it better manners. It does not come into this story.

How close was England to the vital, progressive Continent, which was inventing Universities and rediscovering the Roman Law in a dozen linked centres, from Salerno to Paris? It is hard to pronounce on this, for we cannot tell whether the casual notices which have come down to us relate striking exceptions or everyday occurrences. An English ship called at Genoa, and this seems to be news; yet no one would go all the way by sea from England to Genoa unless he was carrying something very heavy; there was in the port a permanent colony of English merchants, who presumably had come overland. When the Greek Emperor Alexius Comnenus wished to send a polite message to King Henry I of England there was in Constantinople an Englishman ready to carry it; he also brought to the Abbey of Abingdon the right arm of St. John Chrysostom, which was presumably what he had gone to fetch. The life and death of Thomas Becket was made into a saga in Iceland, and painted on the wall of a church at Zamora in Spain, within a few years of his death. There were enough Englishmen in the schools of Paris for some rude songs to be made about their heavy drinking and about the ridiculous tails they did their best to conceal.

That was the world into which young Thomas was born; the Saracens had been driven from Jerusalem, men were building cathedrals which are still the wonder of posterity, at last the Church had been granted her rightful place in society. It was a good time to be born.

It was also a very happy fate to be born a Norman; the world was visibly and obviously getting better every year, and most of the improvements were due to Norman courage, Norman efficiency, Norman ability to lay down a sensible code of rules and enforce them. Fifty years ago had died the last King of England of the old line which went back to Cerdic of Wessex and Woden the heathen god; the childless Edward the Confessor bequeathed his Kingdom to the Duke of Normandy, his great-nephew on his mother's side; when Harold Godwinsson attempted —without a shadow of hereditary right—to seize power for himself, Duke William defeated Harold's personal following at Hastings, and received the Crown of England, from the hands of Ealdred, Metropolitan of York in Westminster Abbey, in a more or less regular way. Of course William the Conqueror promised to rule by the Law of King Edward; that Law had not been made by the holy King; it was the Law of the English, as old as the English race, and it could not be altered by human hands. But equally of course English law could not apply to his Norman followers, who had their own ancient code which no human power could alter. As one English magnate after another lost his estates for unsuccessful rebellion the ruling class became more and more Norman, until in 1086, when Domesday Book was compiled, nearly every manor which did not belong to the King or the Church was in Norman hands.

So Norman barons held the land of England, and of course the land of Normandy. But that was not all; one of their favourite saints was St. Michael the Archangel, patron of warriors, and in the eleventh century many of them made pilgrimage to his shrine at Monte Gargano in southern Italy; the local inhabitants called in these Norman pilgrims to help them in the confused and incessant wars which were fought between the cities, the Lombard aristocracy which once had overrun them, the Byzantine Catapan who represented the Greek Emperor in Constantinople, and the Saracens of Sicily who sometimes raided right up to Rome. By this time the Normans had beaten all their competitors, and the Norman King of Sicily ruled all Italy south of Rome.

It was these Normans of Italy who played the most valiant part in the successful First Crusade, which freed Jerusalem in 1099. Duke Robert of Normandy was one of the candidates for the Crown of the Holy Land, and though that went eventually to the House of Flanders Normans held the Principality of Antioch and some of the most important of the rich but perilous fiefs of Outremer, the land Over Sea.

Every King in Christendom was glad to have Norman warriors in his army and Norman clerks to keep his accounts. Scotland was ruled by a native dynasty, but there were many Norman barons to serve it. Normans helped the Spanish Kings to push back the Moslem invader, and fought for the Count of Oporto before ever there was a Kingdom of Portugal. By the time this book ends the vanguard of the Geraldines will have appeared in Ireland. A sycophant wrote of King Henry II that he knew every language spoken between London and Jerusalem; if he meant that the King understood Serbo-Croat and Wallachian he was talking nonsense; but the northern French of Normandy, plus the southern French of Languedoc, would take a traveller right through the Christian world, and if he was a Norman he would find cousins wherever he stopped for the night.

The Normans were, naturally, very proud of themselves. But they were not exclusive. Anyone who fought gallantly under Norman leadership became an honorary member of the race. The historians of the First Crusade have much to say of the exploits of the Normans of Italy, and we are a little surprised when we discover that the native language of some of the common soldiers was Arabic. The fleet from Winchelsea which liberated Lisbon from the Moors in 1147 cannot have contained many genuine Normans. At the Battle of the Standard, in 1138, the Yorkshire levies were exhorted in the conventional eve-of-battle speech of encouragement by their leader, who happened to be the Norman Bishop of Orkney. He addressed them as 'unconquerable Normans', and reminded them that their cousins had stormed Palermo and Bari, Antioch and Jerusalem; they were certain to defeat the naked and barbarous men of Galloway. And of course they did, though the few Norman knights in the Scottish army, led by Prince Henry, broke their ranks. You note that the Scottish Prince had a Norman name, and of course he fought in the Norman manner.

It was not only on the battlefield that the Normans excelled. They went everywhere, and wherever they went they came to the top. The best lawyers, the best architects, the best business men, the best farmers, the best administrators of a realm or a prosperous estate, were

Norman; there was nothing they could not do, and do better than any foreigner, and they knew it. But their self-confidence was in fact matched by their ability.

The world in which they lived gave scope for their talents. Wise and holy men had worked out the rules on which civilization should be based; these rules were universally admitted to be true, they had been put into practice, and in practice they were proving a success.

We know these rules as Feudalism. The essence of it was that no one owns land absolutely, for all land is held by some service, to be taken away if the service is not performed. In theory the service might be a mere payment of money, but usually it is some action, following your lord to battle if you are free, working for him if you are a serf. It was always carefully delimited; whatever lawyers might say about a serf being the same as a slave every field in England was held because the occupier did so many days' work in the week for his lord, and the hours of each day were laid down; they were fixed by law, and law cannot be altered; they might not be increased, though the manor-court of his fellow peasants kept a slacker up to the mark. In consequence the amount of work demanded for the use of a virgate of fertile land varied in the most surprising way from one village to the next. The other universal obligation was to take your disputes to the lord's court, for the lord was entitled to the money penalties paid by wrongdoers. (Imprisonment was not normally the penalty for a crime, because the feeding of prisoners is a useless expense, and everybody was too busy to guard them; in those days it was held that really wicked men should be killed as soon as possible, and for lesser offences money was the remedy.) A few great lords had the power of life and death, but usually only the King's judges could hang a felon; even then his land was forfeit to his lord, though his moveable property, his chattels, went to the King who sentenced him.

The lord did not own his land absolutely. If he was a simple knight he paid for it by fighting under his over-lord's banner, at his own expense, for so many days in the year. (The forty days given in most books is probably an underestimate, applying only to castle-guard in time of peace; in any case, public opinion expected the vassal to fight for as long as he was needed; but after a certain period he would receive pay and rations.) He was responsible for law and order on his land, and his tenants might appeal to the overlord if he denied them justice; which does not mean giving a wrong judgement, but neglecting to take any steps when the peace is broken. Also if he had a dispute with another free landholder it must be judged in the court of the defendant's overlord, who will receive the penalty.

The theory may most easily be explained by an ex-ample. Supposing in the year 1118 you had come on a peasant ploughing a field, and you asked him whose field it was. He would answer, 'It's my land. I hold it by the service of three days' work every week, from dawn to dinner-time, on the demesne of Sir Ralph over there. At haysel and harvest I must work for him till dark, but then he must give me my dinner. And of course I must attend his court.'

If you then asked Sir Ralph he would answer, 'It's my land. I hold it by knight-service from Count Roger. I follow his banner in war for sixty days at my own ex-pense, and after that for as long as he pays me. In peace

I must ride with him for forty days at my own expense, supposing he wants to make an impressive show at some great council. He has the right to marry my infant heir to any partner he chooses, and the same with my widow, if I should happen to die young. And of course I attend his court.'

If you asked Count Roger he would answer, 'It's my land. I hold it from the King himself, by the usual knight-service. He's a greedy lord, and his aids and reliefs are heavier than anything I dare impose on my own tenants; but at least he's the King, and even a man of my birth may serve him with honour. And of course if I happen to get involved in a lawsuit I have the privilege of going straight to his court.'

If you asked the King he would answer, 'It's my land. I hold it as long as I keep the promises I made at my Coronation. If I broke them too badly all my tenants would combine against me, and I have not enough paid soldiers to suppress rebellion. Things would be much easier if I could get that ploughman before my court. One day I shall, but at present I dare not offend the mesne lords in between, who are jealous of their right of juris-diction.'

It was a good system, so long as the lesser tenants were in fact less important than their lords. Unfortunately the rules of inheritance presently made nonsense of it; be-cause every lady, on her marriage, was given some por-tion of her father's land, and brotherless ladies usually got the whole, in a few generations men were holding scraps of land here and there from many different lords. Richard de Lucy, the Justiciar, held land of the Archbishop of Canterbury; but he held so much more from the King that there was never any prospect of his carrying out the obligations of his homage to the Archbishop. The Bishop of Bayeux owed sixty knights to the King of France, and a hundred knights to the Duke of Normandy; since these two potentates were usually at war he could often escape doing service to either. In King John's day the great William Marshal did liege homage to the King of England and to the King of France, and had to hide in Ireland to avoid fighting for one of his lords against the other; but he also held of a less important baron, William de Braoze, and could succour him when he was a fugitive from the wrath of King John on the excuse that he was only doing his duty to his lord. Feudalism worked so long as one man held one fief; the later accumulation of estate destroyed its meaning.

But while it lasted, and that covers the twelfth century, it had this great advantage, that it put the responsibility for keeping order on the landlord, who had local knowledge and the power to enforce his judgements; and in the profits of justice it gave him an incentive to do his duty.

So far we have spoken chiefly of criminal law and the keeping of order. There was a parallel system, which affected the daily life of the ordinary man more closely. When William the Conqueror took over the governing of England he was shocked to discover that Bishops and sheriffs sat side by side in the Shire Courts, trying every case as colleagues. It was wrong for a layman to try cases which might involve detailed legal knowledge; it was equally wrong for a Bishop to try cases which might end in a sentence of death or mutilation, since Bishops are forbidden by the laws of the Church to shed blood. So each Bishop was ordered to set up a court of his own, where he judged anything that had to do with religion. The three oddly assorted subjects of Divorce, Probate, and Admiralty are still judged by a special court, set up at the Reformation to take over these ecclesiastical cases. Anything to do with wills was a Church matter, because wills are a Roman invention, unknown to the barbarians who overthrew the Empire; when a barbarian died his property was divided among his kin, and the living possessor had no say in what became of it after his death. The Church knew the old Roman rules, and was also deeply interested in wills because it is much easier to persuade a man to leave his wealth to pious or charitable uses than to get it out of him while he is alive to enjoy it; most of the endowments of the Church came by legacy.

Anything to do with marriage was obviously a Church matter. Only the Church could marry, or declare a marriage invalid. There was no divorce, but a great many marriages were slightly invalid because the parties were distantly related; these were good enough to stand while both sides were content, but capable of dissolution if someone was willing to spend a lot of money on a complicated lawsuit.

Disputes on the high seas, where no King rules, are no concern of any King. Normally the parties fought it out until the last man on the losing side was drowned, but if they were willing to argue the Church was willing to hear them. The verdict could not be enforced, and it was nothing more than friendly arbitration; but some people prefer that to war without quarter.

The Church courts also claimed to try any offence committed by a clerk, and this was more reasonable than it sounds, for most clerical offences were not offences against English law. If a clerk habitually went hunting, or made his living by keeping a shop, or ate meat on Fridays, or wore a red gown and a sword, he was not breaking the King's law, but everyone agreed that he ought to be punished for breaking the rules of the Church, the canons, which at the time of his ordination he had freely sworn to obey. The usual punishment was a beating, with a term of imprisonment in a strict monastery (which would resent the extra expense, and give the culprit an uncomfortable time). In extreme cases the court might deprive him of his orders, and make him a layman again. Whether such a heavy punishment, which ruined his career and deprived him of his income, was enough for really serious felonies, was the great matter in dispute between Thomas Becket and the King.

The Church courts could not condemn an offender to death or any punishment involving bloodshed (though Normans did not consider that even the worst flogging drew blood enough to count). Their heaviest sentence was excommunication, but that is a very heavy sentence indeed. While an excommunicate remains under the ban he forfeits all hope of Heaven, and Christians may not associate with him in daily life. But since it is the task of the Church to get sinful Christians into Heaven, not to make their salvation more difficult, an excommunicate might expect absolution, with a more or less stiff penance, as soon as he expressed contrition for his fault; if he was dying he might expect it as a matter of course, for if he died excommunicate he went straight to Hell. Geoffrey de Mandeville was probably the wickedest scoundrel in all the treacherous anarchy of Stephen's reign, but contemporary historians are sorry that he had the bad luck to die excommunicate. The King's courts recognized this sentence; an excommunicate was incapable of suing or taking oath before them; if after forty days he had taken no steps to get himself absolved he became outlaw, and his land escheated to his lord while his chattels went to the King (but this was the common result of most sentences in most courts, for the profits of justice were an important part of a feudal income).

By this time the simple Church courts of the Conqueror, one in each diocese presided over by the Bishop in person, had proliferated, as all legal systems do when unchecked, into a complicated series. Every archdeacon presided over a local court of first instance, from which an appeal lay to his Bishop; from the Bishop an appeal lay to the Archbishop, and from him to the Pope; but because the Pope had no machinery for inquiring into the truth of disputed matters of fact in some outlying province of Christendom he often commissioned the local Bishop or Metropolitan to try the case as his delegate; even when the Pope took this course the suit had to go first to Rome and then come all the way back again, which made it very expensive. Note that there was no court of appeal for England as a whole; a suit brought before the Bishop of Durham might go on appeal to the Archbishop of York, but from him it went straight to Rome, without passing through Canterbury; and of course the King was left out of it altogether.

Until King Henry raised the subject of felonious clerks nobody minded that clerical offenders were judged only by the Church courts. For by strict Canon Law every case which concerned a clerk, even if he was the injured party, should be brought before the Church court. This had the corresponding advantage that robberies and assaults on the clergy incurred only spiritual penalties, and robbers preferred the certainty of excommunication, with a very good chance of absolution before they came to die, to the risk of being hanged or blinded by the King's court if they failed to get through the Ordeal.

But it seems to be a law of nature that every legal system, finding itself unfettered, attempts to increase its jurisdiction. The archdeacons attempted to suppress sin, even sin committed by laymen, and that made them unpopular. Merchants were glad to take suits about broken contracts to the Church court, which claimed that the breach of a contract must involve perjury, since it had been ratified by oath; the Church enforced the sensible rules of commercial morality which had been invented by the ancient Romans, while the King's court, though it had elaborate rules about the possession and inheritance of land, was very vague about the ownership of money and goods. But when the Church tried to fine laymen for getting drunk, or for working on a holiday, the encroachment was resisted with spirit. And a court of morals offers dangerous opportunities for blackmail. It was common gossip, though such a charge is impossible to prove or refute, that archdeacons or their summoners brought false charges of adultery against the wives of respectable burgesses, and demanded a bribe for dropping the case, which of course would destroy the reputation of a decent housewife even though she were acquitted. There was a general feeling that Church courts were good things for the clergy, but that they ought to leave laymen in peace.

So far we have been talking of Church courts and King's courts as though the Church did not include the

King. But of course it did. The Church Militant on earth consists of all Christians, whether lay or clerk. All the King's subjects were Christian, and the officials who kept his accounts and composed his letters, anyone who did any job which involved reading and writing, would be clerks also. The King's Justice in Eyre might well be an archdeacon, who in his other capacity presided over a Church court and wrote himself stiff letters about the conflict of jurisdiction. There was no law against heresy, because there had never been any heretics in England; but when in 1165 a band of Catharan missionaries tried to found a Group in Oxford they were at once sent into exile by royal decree, and since they were also excommunicated, and therefore no one might offer them food or shelter on their journey, most of them died of exposure by the roadside.

It was for the King to help the Church and for the Church to help the King. If those two interdependent authorities quarrelled things would be very unpleasant.

CHAPTER TWO

CHILDHOOD AND EDUCATION

In 1118, when Thomas was born, England was ruled
by King Henry I, youngest son of the great Conqueror; he was a bit of a tyrant, though he allowed
no one else to tyrannize over his subjects, and all men
agreed that he was a great improvement on his brother.
But there was trouble coming, because his only son had
been drowned at sea and there was no undisputed heir to
succeed him; in 1135, when Thomas was sixteen, the
King died and the trouble came.

But before that Thomas had received his schooling.
The education of his flock was the responsibility of the
Bishop of the diocese; he had to arrange that there were
enough men able to read and write to carry on the necessary business of the world, and in England the supply of
such men was always adequate; the remotest manor-court
found a clerk to keep its record in some kind of dog-
Latin, and if he did not know, or could not remember,
the Latin word for some everyday object he just put a
regular termination on the French word, *purkacia* for
purchase or *drana* for drain, and declined it according to
its place in the sentence. The ability to scribble the alpha-
bet was not possessed by everybody, any more than the
ability to use a typewriter is nowadays; but the two skills
may be compared as about equally common. But the

ability to write clearly and well, so that the message may be read at sight by a stranger, is a different thing, as anyone knows who has tried to read lecture-notes, or the minutes of a committee, written by someone else. The art of writing so clearly that a Missal, say, could be read without hesitation by a strange priest at the altar, was about as rare as the art of painting byelaws on a notice-board is nowadays. When we read that Brother So-and-So wrote all the books for a large monastery we must not think that the other monks could not make out a notice saying Do Not Disturb to stick on the doors of their cells.

Thomas learned to read and write, well enough to read his own writing but perhaps not well enough to make a book, in one of the three grammar schools of the city of London. These schools were licensed by the Bishop, who had to be sure the schoolmasters taught sound Christian doctrine and led a godly life. If the burgesses had allowed the schools to close through lack of support I suppose the Bishop would have taken some action; but what he was really concerned with was the danger of unauthorized teachers setting up 'adulterine' schools and taking the bread out of the mouths of his licensed school teachers. The twelfth century believed in a controlled economy, though no one trusted the King's government to administer the controls.

Thomas would be taught entirely in Latin. The master would speak in Latin, and the boy would be beaten if he answered in any other tongue; he would probably be beaten a good deal anyway, for it was assumed that little boys don't like learning, and that the only way of getting them through the preliminaries is to keep them at it very hard, for long hours every day, under constant threat of the rod. All the rules of grammar had to be learned by heart, and there was no attempt to make lessons interesting.

The grammar schools taught nothing but Latin, no history or mathematics or geography. None of these subjects could be learned until the pupil had mastered Latin, for all the available text-books were written in that language. Only when he could think in Latin could he begin his real education.

Thomas learned enough Latin to write a clear letter, and to speak extempore if he had something to say; but he never became an outstanding scholar. No one would read his letters for their style, and he could never manage the graceful, intricate, but meaningless speeches which were then, and are now, appropriate for ceremonial occasions; when it was proposed that he should preach before the Pope and the assembled Doctors of Christendom, at the Council of Tours in 1163, he begged to be excused because of his unpolished language.

In what tongue did he speak at home? French, certainly, since his father and mother were Normans of Normandy (his mother may have been a native of Caen, but historians disagree). Did he also speak English? I think not, though the matter is doubtful. But English was going through a period of decline. The old language of the Saxon court had been as complicated and highly inflected as Greek, and now that it was no longer written by educated men it was breaking up into a welter of ungrammatical dialects. In 1100 the Anglo-Saxon Chronicle, which was kept at St. Augustine's, Canterbury, was translated into Latin, presumably by the last member of the community who could still understand it; but the rival monastery of Christ Church, Canterbury, prided itself in a typically English way on keeping up old traditions. As late as 1150 a Latin psalter of theirs was 'glossed' in English (that is to say the English meaning was written over each Latin word as it came, without bothering about grammar or the order of the words); and in 1154, when King Henry II came to the throne, he confirmed the privileges of Canterbury in an Anglo-Saxon writ; but he was consciously maintaining a quaint old custom, for the writ follows exactly a similar promise of King Canute in 1020, which I suppose the Archbishop showed him as a model. It was on a par with Prince Albert wearing a kilt at Balmoral, a deliberate concession to the local barbarians.

Of course certain English words crept into the French of England, because they described something peculiar to the island; but a Norman lawyer might write of 'outfang-thief' or 'sac and soc' without knowing English, as in recent times an Englishman might write of dacoits and Zemindars without knowing any Indian language.

Thomas therefore spoke Latin at school and French at home. Probably it was good French, since his parents were French-born; for already the French of England was beginning to diverge from the French of France; Guarnier, who wrote about 1180, boasts that he uses correct French because he was born in France, not in England.

We know practically nothing about Thomas as a child. His many contemporary biographers did not include anyone who had played with him outside the walls of London, skating in winter, playing a very rough kind of all-in football, or holding mock jousts against the pages and servants of the King's household at Westminster. But we know that was how young Londoners amused themselves.

Apparently in the 1130s Gilbert Becket was prosperous, one of the leading men of the city; though at the end of his life he was impoverished because accidental fires, the great menace to wooden towns, had destroyed many of the houses on whose rents he lived. Thomas was an only son; he had two sisters, of whom one married a London merchant and the other took vows and eventually became Abbess of Barking; we know that because thirty years later the King sent them into banishment with all the rest of the Becket family; but Thomas does not seem to have met them after he had left the home of his parents.

His mother was devout, and taught him a special devotion to Our Lady; she lived until he was twenty, and she must have implanted in him those habits of piety which remained with him to the end, but which evidently did not come naturally to his reckless character. When Thomas was dead and famous all his friends racked their memories for anecdotes about him; but nothing has come down to us about his ever befriending a stray puppy, or fighting a bully bigger than himself, or doing anything else that would win him credit with the modern Boy Scouts. He was a competent pupil, and he probably behaved himself in class, for his teachers liked him in after life.

The social position of the Becket family is worth investigation: fitzStephen says that Gilbert was of knightly stock, and possibly he was the younger son of a knight; though he himself was never called knight, in a period when that title was used very freely. But a well-to-do burgess of London with a comfortable house had one great social advantage. The King, though he was constantly on the move, visited Westminster more often than any other place, and the barons of the Exchequer were beginning to make it their permanent address; lords and sheriffs, when they had to pay money to the King, would come up to London and stay there while they argued over their accounts. But the inns of London, though they were famous for good cooking, did not furnish sleeping accommodation, or at least sleeping accommodation fit for gentlemen. Important visitors to London would lodge with a substantial burgess. The host could hardly present a bill at the end of his guest's stay; in the twelfth century, when the duty of hospitality was practically unlimited, that would have been considered low; but the lord would be under an obligation to the burgess, and would offer him some favour in return. Madam Becket (there are different versions of her Christian name, which may have been Mahault) must have kept a good cook, for several eminent noblemen always lodged with the Beckets when business called them to town. They would of course dine with the family, and talk together in the French of Normandy; probably there was a good deal of solidarity among the Normans of London, surrounded by English, as nowadays in the Far East traders and government officials who would never meet at home frequent the same club.

Gilbert Becket had the entry to one very distinguished circle. As a child in Thierceville he had played with another village boy, Theobald, who entered a monastery and became eventually Archbishop of Canterbury. They remained friends, and there was always a welcome for Gilbert at the manor of Harrow, which belonged to the Archbishop and where he often stayed.

A constant visitor to the London house was Sir Richer

de l'Aigle, a baron who held large fiefs in the south of England. He took a fancy to little Thomas, and had him to stay at Pevensey Castle in the holidays. (The holidays came at harvest time, when every activity ceased except the urgent work of getting in the corn; if the harvest failed the district would go hungry, for corn was too heavy to transport on the bad roads of those days.) This made a great difference to Thomas in after years. He was taught to ride like a knight and a gentleman, a difficult business; it was held that if a boy couldn't ride by the time he was seven it was impossible to teach him later. He also learned the very complicated and technical craft of hunting with hawks. One of the very few anecdotes of his early life relates how, following his hawk, he put his horse at a footbridge which spanned a mill stream; the bridge was too narrow, and the horse fell in; Thomas, his head muffled in his hood (perhaps it was raining), was swept helplessly towards the mill-wheel, which would cut him to pieces. By good fortune, or possibly by miracle, the miller at that moment left his house to stop the wheel; he saw Thomas, and fished him out unharmed. If you should ever go hawking, and your hawk will not return to your lure and is in danger of being lost, St. Thomas is the saint to call on for help; he used to be very annoyed when it happened to him, and he will sympathize.

So, by a fortunate combination of circumstances, at ten years old Thomas knew his Latin grammar thoroughly, and he also possessed the social accomplishments of a young gentleman who had never deigned to go to school, but had picked up the trade of a knight in the stables and the tilt-yard. In later life he was sensitive about his father's plebeian nickname; he wished to be known as Thomas of

London, and only his enemies called him Becket. But though these enemies raked up every accusation they could think of no one ever accused him of vulgar manners. It was the age which invented heraldry, and men were acutely conscious of their social position; but Thomas was at home in the highest society. He must have been very grateful to Sir Richer de l'Aigle.

It was time to decide on his future career. At ten he was old enough to earn his living, and his skill at reading and writing fitted him for a position in the office of some merchant. He was a devout Christian and attended Mass regularly, but at this time he seemed to have no special vocation for the religious life. If Gilbert had been poor, anxious for his son to support himself as soon as possible, Thomas might have learned a trade, passed a respectable life as a burgess of London, and been buried beside his parents in St. Paul's Cathedral without ever making a name in the world. But his father was still well-to-do, and I suppose the teachers in the grammar school recommended further education for a promising pupil. He was sent to board with the Augustinian Canons at Merton in Surrey.

Of course he went there as a layman, and took no vows. But he was now definitely committed to the clerical life. There were plenty of openings in the secular world for a learned man, but it so happened that all learned men must be paid by the Church, even if they worked for a layman. Kings and great barons needed skilled clerks, but kings and great barons had no regular income in money with which to pay salaries. They could reward their supporters with land, but a fief must be held by knight-service, and most clerks could not fight. Yet all over England the advowson of every church, the right of presenting a clerk to fill the living and draw the tithes, was in the hands of the layman who claimed to be heir to the original builder of the church. You made your steward or secretary Rector of some rich living, and he hired a poor priest to do the work cheaply, as Vicar. It was a bad system, but it was the only way of giving a clerk a yearly income without at the same time giving him an estate which would descend to his heirs for ever, long after he had ceased to work for you.

A layman could not hold a benefice; there would be objections from the Bishop, leading ultimately to excommunication, if the patron gave it to someone who had no orders at all. But the Rector need not be a priest, though he was paid for doing priestly work. Nowadays no one accepts minor orders unless he intends to become a priest; but at that time anyone proposing to earn his living by his brain, or to lead a life of study, took minor orders, perhaps up to exorcist or doorkeeper, without intending to go any further; or he might become a 'tonsured clerk', which meant that he wore on the top of his head a shaven patch; but in any of these events he would have no power to administer the Sacraments, no daily office to recite, in fact no religious duties to perform. Public opinion preferred that he should stay unmarried, and if he took a wife such a disgraceful action might spoil his career. The Pope was always issuing commands that no clerk might marry in any circumstances. In fact they did, especially in England where it had been the custom in Saxon times; sometimes even priests married in England; and if the married priest held a benefice it was likely to be inherited by his son, in accordance with the general custom that all property should be hereditary. (The Westmorland farmer who said, hearing the poet Wordsworth was dead, that he supposed his son would carry on the business, spoke with the true voice of the middle ages.) If a clerk who was only exorcist held a cure of souls for many years, paying a vicar to do the work, the Bishop might in the end inquire when he proposed to proceed to the priesthood. But there was a cast-iron answer. He had only to say he was still completing his education. There was a canon of the Church which allowed any clerk to hold a benefice while studying in the Schools; and as the advanced degrees could only be taken after seventeen years' residence that excuse would last most men until they died of old age.

As a tonsured clerk Thomas would put all thought of marriage behind him, and he would be bound by the canons which forbade clerks to earn a living by buying and selling, or to go hunting for pleasure (though they might kill game for food), or to ride armed. But some of these rules, though they existed, seem to have been a dead letter; as we shall see, Thomas broke most of them, and though he repented of many of the deeds of his youth he never expressed contrition for his hunting and fighting as a deacon.

The pupils at Merton, though they took no vows, would wear the black habit of the Augustinian Canons that the cloister might not be defiled with unseemly and frivolous dress. Augustinian Canons are practically monks —they take the vows of chastity, poverty, and obedience, and say a daily office in choir. But because most of them as priests, may take charge of vacant parishes and preach wherever they are needed, they do not lead such enclosed lives as true monks. Even in those days the perennial shortage of clergy in England was a problem; the Augustinians helped to fill the gap, and kept their rule honestly; they were a respected and popular order.

At Merton Thomas would learn rhetoric. Grammar was the science of writing and speaking Latin according to the rules; but rhetoric was the art of speaking it fluently, wittily, and convincingly, a more difficult task which can only be learned by practice. Later in his career he would have to study divinity, the highest science of all and at that time a most exciting one. The great theologians were laying down the principles on which the later schoolmen built such a magnificent structure; the depths were not yet explored, and anyone might discover some as yet undefined truth. But Thomas was not interested. He never wrote a theological treatise, or used any theological argument which he might not have learned with his prayers at his mother's knee. He knew that the Pope, the successor of St. Peter, held the keys of Heaven and Hell, and that all Christians must obey his mandates. He did not inquire further.

He must have been happy at Merton, for in after life he held the community in great affection, and made it his business to see it richly endowed. His teacher was Prior Robert of Merton, and years later Prior Robert of Merton was his confessor. But we must beware of the lack of surnames; this second Prior Robert was probably his school-fellow and contemporary, not his old teacher.

On the 1st of December 1135 King Henry I died suddenly, and that affected the whole realm. For the next nineteen years there was a disputed succession, and though on the whole King Stephen, grandson of the Conqueror and nephew of Henry I, held most of the country for most of the time, he could not govern as firmly as his predecessors. We are apt to exaggerate the ensuing anarchy. The accident that one very vivid writer lived in the Fens, where Geoffrey de Mandeville really let himself go, and that another wrote of neighbouring barons striking their own coinage, which only happened in Yorkshire, gives false emphasis to the picture. The Thames valley was in the front line, with Stephen based on London and Matilda based on Bristol, but over most of the country monasteries were founded, churches were built, and local courts dispensed justice. The lands of a strong lord might even prosper the more because the King dared not collect all his aids and taxes.

Two sections of the community actually gained in strength and prestige. Both Matilda and Stephen appealed to the Pope; this gave an opportunity to the English Bishops, who got into the habit of meeting together to throw the whole weight of the Church on the side of the ruler who promised them the most freedom, especially the freedom to communicate with Rome without first seeking royal permission. In 1136 King Stephen promised that Bishops should have jurisdiction over all cases concerning ecclesiastics; this was enrolled as the third Statute of the Realm. The Church faced the King boldly, because whoever was rightful King of England there was no doubt that Theobald was Archbishop of Canterbury; he held the mightiest position in England which was also unquestioned.

The second institution which profited by anarchy was the City of London. There was as yet no mayor, but the Londoners must have enjoyed some form of self-government; and their power of quickly raising large sums of ready money made them worth courting in a war fought chiefly by paid mercenaries.

Meanwhile Thomas had gone abroad to complete his education at the School of Paris; these schools attached to cathedrals were presently to turn into universities, and indeed the older School of Bologna was on the verge of being organized as a university, specializing in teaching Law. But Bologna had come into being as a club of students hiring learned men as teachers, and therefor was governed by undergraduates; a student might cut his lectures unrebuked, but a professor was heavily fined if he was late in the lecture-hall. In consequence it was a rowdy place, unsuitable for lads in their teens. Paris began as a club of teachers, who dovetailed their lectures into a complete course of study; therefore the dons had some power of discipline, even though English students sometimes fought their German colleagues with bows and daggers, or both combined to rob the lay townsmen; for every student at the Schools was automatically a clerk.

Paris specialized in theology, but other subjects were taught there. I think Thomas studied chiefly Canon and Roman Law; at least that was what he knew best in after life, though later he studied the subject elsewhere.

He did not take a degree. You must pass seventeen years of disputation in the schools before you might hope to be regarded as a learned doctor; but you would take no examination; it would be assumed that if you had hung about the place all that time you must have picked up a great deal of learning. Even a Master's degree took longer than the three years which is the most Thomas could have spent in Paris. But the dates for this part of his life are vague. It is evident that he enjoyed himself, and afterwards remembered his student days with pleasure. When he visited Paris as King Henry's ambassador he befriended the English students, and as Chancellor he saw that his old tutor, Robert of Melun, was made Bishop of Hereford (Robert was called of Melun because he had taught there, but he was of Anglo-Norman birth).

When Thomas was about twenty his mother died and he came home. In London he found his father impoverished by a fire which had destroyed many of his houses, and it must have been suggested that the time had come for the young man to earn his living. The picture is familiar; the devoted mother who cannot believe that her darling boy is really grown up, and wishes him to continue his education; and the stern father, who cannot see that his son has brains out of the ordinary, and holds that the sooner he goes to work the sooner he will have the nonsense knocked out of him.

Thomas must have been hard to please. For a year he lived in idleness looking for a post worthy of his talents. This cannot have been because no one offered him a job; a young student fresh from the Schools of Paris looking for employment in the London of 1140 would be like a young graduate of the Massachusetts Institute of Technology looking for work in a modern factory. Employers would compete for him.

Evidently Thomas wanted a really good post in the King's household, or on the staff of some important Bishop. But these posts were normally held for life, and I suppose there was no vacancy. At last the pressure of poverty was too much for his pride, and he entered the office of a London merchant. His employer was a Nor-

man named Osbert, with the added nickname of Huitdeniers, or Eightpence, presumably earned by some lucky
stroke of business. We do not know what the business
was, but it involved writing letters to foreigners, and
therefore in Latin, the international language. Some biographers said that Thomas was clerk to the Corporation
of London; but as yet there was no Corporation, and the
basis for this mistake is that in 1141 Osbert Huitdeniers
was one of the four 'viscounts' who administered the city.
'Viscount' is a vague word, which could be the equivalent of sheriff; in this connection it probably means magis-
trate of the city court, and leader of the city militia. Perhaps during the civil war the Londoners had won the
right of electing these viscounts; perhaps they were appointed by whichever claimant held London. It is worth
noting that 1141 was the year in which Matilda entered
London, after Stephen had been captured at the battle of
Lincoln. If she appointed Osbert, who was a friend of the
Beckets, it suggests that Gilbert was a supporter of the
Angevin faction; a reason why Henry II should be friendly
with Thomas later.

But London as a whole favoured Stephen. Matilda retired without being crowned by the Archbishop of Canterbury in Westminster Abbey; in consequence she might
never call herself Queen, but only Lady of England
(Domina); Stephen was King, even while he was a
prisoner, because he had been properly crowned. It was
Coronation which made the King, and it must be performed by the right person in the right place; William
Rufus and Henry I were Kings because they had been
crowned, though neither was the true heir of William the
Conqueror. This point will become important when we

find Thomas making a fuss about the irregular Coronation of the eldest son of Henry II.

London was represented at the Council of Winchester in 1141, which tried to end the civil war by a negotiated peace; Osbert must have been an envoy, and presumably he brought his secretary. This would be Thomas's first experience of political affairs, but he was still a junior clerk of twenty-two, and no one recorded his actions for posterity. The Council broke up in disagreement, because there was no armistice while it sat and the strength of the contending parties changed rapidly during the discussion. King Stephen was released in exchange for the Earl of Gloucester, Matilda was driven first from Winchester, then from Oxford, until she was back at her old headquarters in Bristol and King Stephen reigned in London.

By the winter of 1143 Thomas, now very nearly twenty-five, determined to better himself. His elaborate University education was wasted in the counting-house of a merchant, and his only hope of making a name in the world was to find a post in the household of a great magnate. Perhaps his sisters had now left home, one to marry and the other to enter her convent, and there was no further need for him to contribute to their support. He was willing to begin at the bottom, if his new employment offered good prizes at the top.

Archbishop Theobald often visited his favourite manor of Harrow, and while he was there his messengers from the Continent must of course pass through London; they would sleep in the city, to reach him next morning during business hours; for in the twelfth century busy men began work at dawn, even in midsummer, and worked steadily until dinner soon after midday; but nobody read or wrote letters in the evening, since the inefficient and smelly candles of those days were trying to the eyes. It was widely known that if you had business with the Archbishop the place to stop in London was the comfortable house of Theobald's childhood friend, Gilbert Becket, where they kept in touch with the Primate and would give you directions for the road. In particular two brothers, Baldwin archdeacon of Boulogne and Master Eustace (Master in this connection means 'learned in the law') were continually arriving and departing. They prepared the ground, recommending the diligent and energetic clerk as a suitable recruit, and Thomas was expected when he rode out to Harrow.

But he committed one of his rare errors of social behaviour. Apparently Gilbert's house was used as a London hotel by all ranks of the Archbishop's servants, and the man he chose to accompany and guide him held the humble post of woodchopper to the kitchen. When they arrived Thomas happened to be carrying his chopper for him, and he at once earned the nickname of 'Bailhache' or woodchopper from the cheeky young clerks who would be his rivals and comrades. He always resented sneers at his middle-class origin, and this nickname was a nuisance to him in later life.

CHAPTER THREE

ARCHBISHOP THEOBALD

An Archbishop needed a large staff of clerks to conduct his affairs. It is hard to conceive the amount
of sheer physical labour that was necessary in a
busy office where there were no typewriters, no carbon-
paper or other devices for copying, no telephones, and no
regular delivery of mail. If Theobald wished to send a
pastoral letter to be read in each church in his Diocese
every copy must be written separately, by a clerk who
could write clearly, probably in daylight; if he sent an
important message to the King, or the Pope, it must be
delivered by a special messenger, who must wait to ride
back with the answer. If there was business which involved negotiation and bargaining the envoy could not
refer to his principal without riding the whole way back,
and it needed great care, and great foresight, to draw up
instructions which covered every contingency. In fact the
usual way of negotiating at long range was to talk the
matter over with an intelligent and trustworthy young
man, active enough for all the riding involved, and then
give him a sealed paper of credentials, authorizing him to
conclude any agreement in your name. Then he would
be absent for weeks and months, while someone else must
do his work in the office. There was the further point that

the only way in which the Archbishop could draw any profit from his numerous but scattered manors was to visit them each in turn, eating the harvest until it was finished and the time had come to move on to the next; for bad roads made it impracticable to transport the produce of Harrow to Canterbury. Therefore all the business documents, the records of appeals from Diocesan courts, the lists of beneficed clergy and of vacant benefices, the applications for dispensation to permit cousins to marry, must be kept in boxes which could be carried on muleback, and when they were unloaded on arrival there must be someone present who remembered what was in which box. From the earliest times there had been a large 'family' of clerks in the household of the Archbishop.

But Theobald was a famous scholar of the new Canon Law, and he used his 'family' as a training school for clever young men destined to high office in the Church. Thomas's colleagues included John of Salisbury, the eminent humanist who became Bishop of Poictiers, John of Canterbury who became Archbishop of Lyons, and Roger de Pont l'Evêque who became Archbishop of York. All these bright young men were continually in the Archbishop's company, dined at his table, and passed the evenings, when it was too dark for writing, in chatting with him about affairs of state. The relationship was rather like that between a modern General and the A.D.C.s on his staff.

At last we have a description of Thomas's personal appearance, for of course these well-known writers published their memories of him after his death. He was immensely tall (one late record says six foot eleven inches, but I don't believe it); his Mass-vestments were preserved in the Cathedral of Sens until the French Revolution, and worn by the officiating priest on his feast day; the tallest priest in the Cathedral was chosen to wear them, and even then they had to be pinned up. He was also very thin, and like many tall thin men he suffered from a bad circulation; he normally wore a great many clothes, sometimes three times as much as was customary; he ate sparingly, but it had to be well-cooked nourishing food; when he tried to live on the bread and cabbage which was the sole diet of the monks at Pontigny he became very ill, and was forced to go back to his chickens and beefsteak. He was dark, with black hair and a great beak of a Norman nose. His hearing was exceptionally acute, and he was lucky enough to have very good eyesight which remained perfect up to his death; that was important in the days before spectacles had been invented, when a scholar whose eyes failed him would be compelled to give up reading. All his senses served him well, including that of taste; he was a good judge of wine, able to name the vintage at the first sip; but he did not particularly care for it, and his favourite drink is described by a puzzled contemporary as 'water in which hay had been boiled'; evidently the French *tisane* made from lime-blossom or other herbs in the manner of modern tea; perhaps he had picked up in Paris a habit unknown in England.

This tall, big-nosed, black-haired, keen-sighted hunter and horseman must have seemed more like one of the Norman knights who had vanquished ten times their number of infidels at Antioch than like the other sedentary and pious clerks of the Archbishop. In fact, though for most of his life he fought with spiritual weapons he was fundamentally a warrior, usually insisting on leading a gallant charge by himself while his commander was anxious to discuss terms of peace.

He developed late; it was five years since he had left Paris, and those five years had been wasted in a London counting-house. But at twenty-five, with his mother dead and his father apparently not very friendly, he was mature. Most of his colleagues liked him, though Roger de Pont l'Evêque was rubbed the wrong way; Roger stuck to the nickname of 'Bailhache' and made fun of him all his life. But the others found him willing and energetic, ready to do his share of the work and capable of doing it properly. He was tactful and polite; his manners were excellent, and in negotiation he was quick-witted enough to give way gracefully if need be, never causing bad blood by arguing a losing case to the bitter end.

But there is one thing to be noticed. Although he was popular in the crowd of busy officials he did not make one intimate friend; three volumes of his correspondence have come down to us, but all deal with business matters; he never chatted with a friend on paper, although that was a common habit of the middle ages and John of Salisbury, for example, spent many hours at it. There is a story that when a group of students in Paris were choosing the ladies whom they would serve, after the new fashion of chivalry, Thomas volunteered that he had chosen Our Lady; he made his devotions faithfully, and there was never a secular love-affair in his life; but the impression he made was of a cold, self-centred man who in fact was serving Thomas of London and nobody else. As I see it, he was a warrior who had not yet enlisted; he had not found the cause and the leader for which he wished to do battle with all his fierce Norman energy and courage.

The Archbishop of Canterbury was a very busy man, all the more because he was constantly negotiating to end the civil war in England. About this time he visited the Pope in Rome, and Thomas may have gone with him. Later Thomas was sent by himself to prosecute an appeal before the Papal Curia. This, the Pope's household of Cardinals and other officials, was the final court of appeal in every ecclesiastical case; but it was more than a final court of appeal, because either party, at any stage of the proceedings before an archdeacon or a Diocesan Bishop, might stop the suit by appealing to Rome. If the case was important, and was obviously going to end there, it saved expense in the long run if you appealed as soon as possible. You might even appeal in advance, before the case had been opened, on the ground that you knew the character of your Bishop and were morally certain that whatever he decided would be wrong. Quite small cases went all the way to Rome; Richard of Anstey left a record of his litigation about this time, and the question of whether his uncle, who left one manor in Berkshire, had been validly married was decided by the Roman Curia.

The Roman Curia was more popular with lawyers than with their clients. The Cardinals were well-trained in the fascinating new subject of Canon Law, and it was an intellectual treat to plead before them; their verdicts were usually sound, unless there were important reasons of foreign or domestic policy for favouring one side against the other. But the fees and costs were enormous; for Rome was a squalid ruin, sacked at frequent intervals by Guelfs or Ghibellines, or both, and the officials of the Curia could only live by overcharging their suitors. Public opinion believed that the longest purse always won, but this may have been the malicious gossip of the unsuccessful.

Roman and Canon Law was the latest and most interesting branch of learning, as new and exciting as atomic physics to-day. The laws of Justinian had recently been rediscovered, and since Justinian, in the sixth century, was the last Emperor of Constantinople to rule in Rome also, and the last to write in Latin instead of Greek, it was plausible to hold that his laws were still the law of the Holy Roman Empire. In Bologna Canon Law, hitherto a mass of undigested and conflicting precedents, was being established by Gratian as a special study; soon his *Decretum* would have to be read by every ambitious clerk.

This study suited Thomas. There was no sentimentality about it; some things were wrong, and others right, without half-shades or moral exhortation. Though the law did not cover every case it laid down general principles from which an intelligent man could draw convincing conclusions. Thomas did well in Rome, and afterwards was sent to attend lectures in Auxerre and Bologna; when he returned he must have had a first-class training in both Roman and Canon Law.

Archbishop Theobald evidently considered he would make a good lawyer; but that is not, perhaps, the very highest compliment that can be paid to a young clerk. The Archbishop, who had been a very holy monk, did not think much of ecclesiastical lawyers as a class, and the public opinion of the time agreed with him. But he must have admired Thomas for his intelligence, even if he did not see in him the zeal of potential sanctity. The young clerk naturally lived at the Archbishop's expense while he was abroad, and the lecturers' fees would amount to a considerable sum. We do not know how he divided his time between Bologna and Auxerre; but in the Schools of Paris he would have studied the leading textbooks written on the subject, and this short course would enable him to hear the latest ideas of the most eminent Doctors. There was not time enough for him to take a degree, but henceforward it would be polite to call him *Master* Thomas of London, the learned lawyer.

In 1148 there was a brush between the Church and the secular government. The King had been imprisoning those Bishops, not very holy men, who had played him false in the civil war; the Pope called a Council at Rheims, chiefly to arrange the affairs of the Second Crusade, but incidentally to threaten Stephen with interdict or excommunication. Naturally the Archbishop of Canterbury was summoned to attend; but William the Conqueror had laid down that no tenant-in-chief of the Crown might cross the sea without the King's permission. (This was quite a sensible rule; no baron could render his military service if he was abroad when the army was mustered.) Stephen chose to enforce the rule against Theobald, who of course was a baron among his many other functions; though it had never been intended that a King should prevent a Bishop from obeying a summons to visit the Pope. Theobald, an elderly man who had lived a sheltered life, very bravely crossed the Channel by stealth in a small open boat. Thomas was with him at Rheims, but apparently he did not share his dangerous voyage; an unimportant clerk, who held no land, might visit Rheims without seeking anyone's permission.

At first the King was extremely angry at this open defiance, but Theobald easily won forgiveness by the part he played in the Council. St. Bernard, the most influential clerk in Christendom, was all for immediate excommunication; but the Archbishop spoke up for his sovereign, for whom there was much to be said; if Bishops defend castles and lead armies they must expect to be treated as prisoners of war when they are beaten. The case against King Stephen was adjourned, and never reopened.

For his defiance Theobald was formally exiled, which meant that he stayed on in Rheims, an honoured guest of the French; by the end of the year (the Council was held in March) he was back in Canterbury.

This exciting episode, which he saw at close quarters, must have made a deep impression on Thomas. An Archbishop defied his King and received sentence of exile, as Anselm and other Archbishops had been exiled in the past. Then the public opinion of Christendom declared itself unmistakeably, and after the King had climbed down all was forgiven and forgotten. This precedent must have been at the back of his mind when later he defied King Henry. But it was a thoroughly misleading precedent; King Stephen was not King Henry, and the Archbishop was not the benevolent and rather woolly-minded Theobald, who defended his enemy before the tribunal of his friend, but a professional lawyer with an unforgiving temper.

King Stephen, a gallant warrior but a stupid politician, continued to be victorious in the long-drawn civil war, but he could never conciliate his defeated enemies or keep in order his boisterous supporters. He had gradually muddled himself into a silly dispute about the Archbishopric of York, and thus incurred the hostility of the whole Church; he had hoped to see his son Eustace crowned in his lifetime, but the Pope would not permit it, and when Eustace died in August 1153 he had nothing more to plan for. He sought peace at almost any price. He had another son, William, who was Earl of Warenne under the Angevins; but no one took William seriously. In the twelfth century, when the score or so of magnates who governed England met constantly at councils and tournaments, and knew one another very intimately, you sometimes find this unanimous agreement that Earl So-and-So is too feeble to be used even as a figurehead; Norman nobles were too practical to waste their time on the equivalent of Richard Cromwell.

King Stephen was old and sick and disappointed; all he wanted was to end his days as a crowned King. In November 1153 he concluded a treaty with young Henry, Matilda's son, by which he kept England for his life and recognized Henry as his heir. Matilda was still alive, but the great argument of her opponents had been that a woman could not rule a Kingdom; now Henry was old enough to rule by himself, and the Treaty of Winchester passed her by. For the first time since 1135 the land was at peace.

In 1154 Thomas, now thirty-five, won promotion to the summit of his profession. He was appointed archdeacon of Canterbury. The archdeacon presided over the episcopal court, and to Canterbury an appeal lay from all the suffragan courts of the Province. The only court above it was the Curia of Rome, the highest court in the world. He would be kept very busy, and he might expect to hold his great position for life. Theobald had nominated only two archdeacons during his long tenure of the Primacy; the first, in accordance with a charming medieval custom which has left traces in the present day, was his own brother; when he was made Bishop of Rochester, Roger de Pont l'Evêque, Thomas's early rival, had been chosen; now Roger was Archbishop of York. Thomas also might expect a Bishopric, but as a way of giving him a dignified pension when he was too old for work. Everyone knew he was a lawyer first and foremost, too worldly to make a good Bishop.

In the Primitive Church the deacon distributed the alms of the faithful. Because he gave alms he collected subscriptions, then the voluntary subscriptions became compulsory dues; until by this time, besides his work as a judge, the archdeacon was the financial agent and business manager of his Diocese. He lived on horseback, constantly inspecting churches and clergy, which is why nowadays he wears gaiters as riding-dress. It was his job to see that everyone who owed money to the Bishop paid up promptly, and debt-collecting always makes a man unpopular. To add to the unpleasantness, he was entitled to hospitality from the parochial clergy whom he was inspecting, and if he chose to travel in great state he could put them to considerable expense; a generation later the archdeacon of Richmond (Yorks) expected his unwilling hosts to feed 97 horses, 21 hounds, and 3 hawks; but this was overdoing it, and he was rebuked by Pope Innocent III. The official allowance was then fixed at 7 horses; but I expect Thomas travelled with a great many more.

The wits of the Schools made fun of the money-grubbing preoccupations of an archdeacon; a favourite subject they debated in the taverns was the question whether an archdeacon could hope to enter Heaven, and it was usually answered in the negative. Everyone agreed that the fabric and vestments of churches should be the most splendid things in the world, and that holy men should be very free with their alms to the poor; the archdeacon, by constant attention to business, collected the wealth which made this possible; he was necessary, but he was a necessary evil, and though powerful he was not respected.

To qualify for his new post Thomas was ordained deacon, one of the lower of the major orders. In order to endow him for the upkeep of the great train of horses he needed for his travels and to pay the many functionaries of his court, he was made rector of St. Mary-le-Strand, London, and of Otford, Kent, cures for which he must have hired vicars, Provost of the great collegiate Church of Beverley, Dean of Hastings, and prebendary of St. Paul's Cathedral in London and of Lincoln Cathedral, dignified sources of income which entailed no particular duties. It was then a common abuse to give a man an important post which carried very little salary, and to make up his income by giving him other well-paid posts which carried no duties, as nowadays the holder of the Privy Seal enjoys a large salary for doing nothing, but is always expected to supervise some particular branch of the administration. Pluralism at that time carried no stigma; people would only think that Thomas of London must be a useful servant of the Archbishop to be so well rewarded.

So in the autumn of 1154 Thomas was at the summit of his legal career, rich, busy, and admired for his efficiency; but not particularly respected for holiness of character, since he had deliberately chosen the most worldly side of the great business of maintaining the Church of Christendom.

CHAPTER FOUR

KING HENRY AND HIS CHANCELLOR

Ring Stephen died on the 25th of October 1154, and the whole country accepted young Henry of Anjou as his rightful heir. But Henry was on the Continent, and for six weeks Archbishop Theobald kept the peace, until by the sacred rite of Coronation the new King was made capable of fulfilling his duties. There was no formal Regency, but in the absence of a King all men expected the Archbishop of Canterbury to take charge.

His new subjects hailed young Henry with unbounded delight. The anarchy had not been a period of unmitigated disaster, and many parts of the country had increased in civilization when the central government relaxed its expensive and stultifying hold; but now everybody was tired of fighting, and in the mood for peace and order. Men wanted legal title-deeds which they could pass on to their children, instead of holding their lands by the sword.

Henry was twenty-one years of age, and already experienced in warfare and government. For more than four years he had kept the peace in Normandy, and since the death of his father in August 1153 he had ruled Maine and Anjou as well. In 1152 he had married Eleanor, Duchess of Aquitaine in her own right, whose previous marriage to the King of France had been annulled by the Pope, technically because they were cousins, in fact because she did not get on with her husband. Eleanor was a good deal older than Henry, and just as obstreperous and bad-tempered; they fought like cat and dog all their married life, and she brought up her sons to make war on their father; but the match brought him the great Duchy of Aquitaine in south-western France, of course under the King of France as suzerain, so that as Duke of Normandy and Aquitaine and Count of Anjou he could ride on his own land from the Channel to the Pyrenees. He was a very great man, even before he became King of England.

The gallant hot-headed warrior of twenty-one must have been rather engaging. His hair was a flaming red, and the light grey eyes which looked out of a freckled weather-beaten face were eager and questing. He ate and drank enormously; but he did not get fat, because he took so much exercise. He often covered in one day what was regarded as a four days' journey, and at the age of forty he rode 140 miles in two days. He was so full of energy that he could never be idle; in fact he preferred to do two things at once, dictating letters while he heard Mass and mending hunting-gear with his own hands while he sat in council. He was passionately fond of hunting, but he also had serious intellectual interests. The famous Greek scholar Adelard of Bath had at one time been his tutor, and he read, for his own pleasure, the latest Latin books on history and politics. He may have been able to write, but a man of his eminence would never pen anything with his own hand; there would be clerks to take dictation. I have already mentioned his alleged knowledge of languages, but it does not appear that he could speak English, though he may have learned by heart a few appropriate expressions of formal politeness.

In contrast to King Stephen, the tallest warrior on the field of Lincoln, he was short and clumsily made; he dressed very shabbily, and his dirty hands with their bitten nails were considered a disgrace to his rank; but he spent lavishly on robes and jewels for state occasions, and when he took the trouble he could look like the great King he was.

There was a legend that long ago an ancestor of the Counts of Anjou had married a fairy, a daughter of the Devil. King Henry never boasted of his diabolic descent, as did his sons in the next generation; but he had inherited the family curse of an uncontrollable temper. Once, in his bedroom, hearing the Justiciar of Normandy tactlessly praise the valour of his enemy the King of Scotland, he first tore off all his clothes and rolled naked on the floor, then pulled the cover off his mattress and chewed the straw filling. His everyday language was unusually coarse and blasphemous; and this in an age which was accustomed to plain speaking, since the monkish chroniclers usually rendered as 'By this and by that' the hair-raising oaths with which every baron punctuated a speech in the King's council.

Henry was madly excited to find himself King of England at the age of twenty-one. In that first winter he rode through the land like a whirlwind, bringing the benefits of law and order to districts which for nineteen years had been ruled by the sword. He had the luck to begin with a perfectly clean slate, for there was no party which wished to bring back the House of Blois, and most of the famous warriors who had fought for his mother were dead; there was neither an opposition to be watched nor a clique of supporters to be rewarded. But he must always bear in mind that the Archbishop of Canterbury had prevented the crowning of Eustace his rival, and had kept the country at peace until he arrived. From gratitude as well as from policy he must allow him great weight in the government. When he needed a trustworthy clerk to fill the most important clerical position in his household he naturally consulted Theobald.

The position was that of Chancellor, the official in charge of the Great Seal of England. In days when most men could not write, and those who could had all been trained to form their letters in the same way, signatures were not used to authenticate documents; every earl, bishop, baron or abbot had a seal which was attached to documents to show he approved of the contents. Some seals were little blobs of wax, dropped on the parchment and only stamped on one side; but the Great Seal of England was a massive affair, like a small printing press. A ribbon would be threaded through the written parchment, then inserted in a lump of several pounds of hot beeswax, an expensive commodity; the counterseal would lie underneath, and the seal proper would be pressed down with wooden screws; when the wax set the design would be impressed on both sides and the document would carry the assent of the King. Much the best way to prove ownership of land or of some right of doing justice was to exhibit a sealed charter from the King; there were other ways, calling evidence that your ancestors had possessed it since the days of William the Conqueror, for example; but that was uncertain and expensive, and in the end the King might not be convinced; there was no arguing against the Great Seal of England.

For this reason it was important that the Chancellor should be honest and diligent. The King had no time to read the masses of documents which issued from his chancery, and if the Chancellor affixed the seal to some letter which did not express the right policy, or worse still, sealed a grant of land for himself or one of his friends, there would be endless trouble before the matter could be put right. The Chancellor must also be a sound scholar. The King would tell him in French the gist of what he must write to the Pope or the Emperor, and the clerks of the chancery must turn it into elegant Latin; or the ignorance of the King of England would be a laughing stock among foreigners. It would also be helpful if the Chancellor had an accurate memory. Copies were kept of all documents which issued from the Chancery; but the whole office, with its archives, accompanied the King on his ceaseless travels, and for convenience these office copies were stitched together, but unlike a modern letter-book, there was no index, and no means of finding any passage in the middle without leafing through the whole thing, and reading on until you came across what you wanted. A Chancellor who could say to his royal master when a case came up for judgement, 'It's no good promising your support to Count X in his claim to the lands of Y. Six months ago I wrote in your name to Count A, saying you considered his claim was better,' would be able to save the King and the rest of the Chancery staff a lot of trouble.

The Chancellor was also in theory the King's personal chaplain, or rather the head of a large staff of personal chaplains. The King would consult him when a Bishopric or important Abbey was vacant; though the King's share in the appointment of Bishops and Abbots is a complicated subject, and I shall deal with the tangled rights of it later in this book.

Finally, as the most important clerk in the King's service, the Chancellor was the chief liaison officer between the parallel administrations of Church and State. The troubles of the reign of Stephen had arisen partly because the King quarrelled with the Church, and Archbishop Theobald was anxious that there should be no such quarrels in future.

For all these reasons Theobald reluctantly parted with the most useful clerk in his household, and recommended Thomas of London, archdeacon of Canterbury, as Chancellor to King Henry. (It is inaccurate to call him Chancellor of England; he was Chancellor of all Henry's possessions, Aquitaine and Normandy as well as the kingdom.)

In January 1155 Thomas received the Great Seal, and it was presumably from this period that he began to know the King personally.

Rather surprisingly, the tall thin dark scholar of thirty-six and the short squat ruddy warrior of twenty-one immediately became bosom friends. They were both lonely, self-centred, and preoccupied with the future, and neither had intimates of older standing to come between them. They had tastes in common, a love of hunting, intellectual curiosity, and a boundless appetite for work. For the first time in his life Thomas need not bother about his career, for he had all the money he needed and the prospect of a Bishopric when he came to retire. Hitherto he had been very decorous, and a little self-important, because it would never do if rivals held his levity up to ridicule; now he might relax.

Since he was fifteen years older than his new friend he might have tried to play the heavy uncle. In fact his happiness made him young, and he joked in public with his lord as though they were cheerful undergraduates together. It was not only during office hours that they were constantly in company; one day they rode through London after a day's hunting, and in Cheapside a ragged beggar asked them for alms; the King said the beggar needed a new cloak, and Thomas agreed; but he pointed out that the King's hunting cloak was too shabby even to give to a beggar. He was always chaffing Henry about his shabbiness.

'Here's a cloak which would make worthy alms, even from a King,' Henry answered, and tried to snatch the gorgeous mantle from his Chancellor's shoulders. Thomas resisted, and the two men wrestled on horseback like riotous young pages, until the escort came up at the gallop, thinking the King in danger. Of course the beggar got the cloak.

Sometimes the comrades would explore the night-life of London, offering to fight the watch when they were commanded to explain their reason for being out after curfew. But they did not get drunk, and though Henry pursued every pretty face his Chancellor, remembering he was a deacon, remained as chaste as a monk. So respectable men did not worry too much.

In one thing they differed. Henry had never been poor, and the necessary state of a King irked him. When he came in from hunting at the early winter dusk, knowing he must kill time by torchlight until he went to bed, he would drop in alone for a chat with Thomas and the clerks who dined at his table. On days when the Chancellor was busy and the King was not he might ride his horse into the office, and even jump it over the table in boyish bravado. He enjoyed turning up unexpectedly to see what Thomas was doing.

But Thomas, the middle-class son of a burgess, who had known poverty as a young man, was thrilled to find himself great, and lived in more splendid state than had ever been seen in a subject. In particular his dress was magnificent, which gives point to the story of the beggar and the cloak. In those days there was no special clerical garb which the clergy must wear outside church, in the manner of the modern dog-collar; but a deacon was expected to dress soberly, avoiding the extremes of fashion, as nowadays an undergraduate is supposed to wear a dark suit under his gown in the examination hall. Thomas outraged public opinion by the extravagance of his clothes; the clergy thought it unbecoming in a deacon, and the laity thought it too splendid for the son of a burgess.

In my opinion Thomas did not think of himself as a deacon, and in the excitement of success he had forgotten he was the son of a burgess. He thought of himself as a knight who had found a worthy lord, one under whose banner he would ride out to set the world to rights. Henry was a gallant knight himself, and he had not been long on the throne before he summoned the knight-service of England to foreign war.

His first war, in January 1156, was a sordid family squabble. Geoffrey, his brother, claimed he had been promised Anjou as a consolation prize when Henry secured

England; if we remember that William Rufus and Henry I had both ousted their brother from the throne we may understand why Geoffrey considered himself entitled to compensation for not being a rival. But Henry always stood up for his full rights as heir to his father, his mother, his maternal grandfather, and his wife. He attacked Geoffrey's Angevin castles, and of course wherever the King went the chancery went also. Thomas was with him when he reduced the important fortresses of Chinon, Mirabel, and Loudon. It was the first campaign Thomas had seen, and presumably he wore mail for the first time; in those days a man of thirty-six was already middle-aged, and he probably kept in the background while he practised the art of jousting; but Richer de l'Aigle had made him a good horseman, and horsemanship was nine-tenths of the skill of a knight.

1157 and 1158 were years of peace, but Thomas played a principal part in two great affairs. The first was a legal dispute between the Bishop of Chichester and the Abbot of Battle, a case which stirred the heart of every Norman, for Battle Abbey was the great Norman war memorial. The Diocese of Chichester still follows the boundaries of the ancient Kingdom of Sussex, and the Abbey lay within it; but William the Conqueror at its foundation had put it under royal protection, and the Abbey claimed this exempted it from obedience to the bishop. For eighty years this had not been seriously challenged, but in 1147 the Pope appointed to the See of Chichester an Anglo-Norman clerk of his Curia, trained in those new theories of church discipline which were more firmly held in Rome than in more outlying provinces of Christendom. The days were passing when Popes would tactfully ignore, or acquiesce in the assumption of powers such as those wielded by the Conqueror over the English Church. For ten years Bishop Hilary had been attempting to make the Abbot swear obedience to him, and now at last, after the usual delays, the case was ready to be heard before the King in person.

Since the King was to hear it the suitors must follow the King on his travels, badgering him to fix a day when they could bring into court their documents and their oathswearers, often disappointed when more urgent business took precedence. That was one reason why litigation was so frightfully expensive. At very short notice the King announced that he would hear the parties at Colchester, where he happened to be in May 1157. Of course the King did not sit alone; every baron was entitled to help him judge his cases, and on this occasion, though no Great Council had been summoned, those magnates who happened to be visiting him were there to give advice. They were not expected to display the impartiality of modern jurymen; they took sides openly from the beginning, and most of them took the side of the Abbot. That was to be expected, for the Abbot of Battle was the brother of Richard de Lucy, Justiciar of England; besides the natural sentiment of all Normans to support the Norman foundation of Battle against the Saxon See of Chichester, the ties of kinship would be working for the monks.

Bishop Hilary, remembering his training in the Roman Curia, opened the proceedings by playing what he considered an unbeatable ace of trumps. He displayed letters from Adrian IV, the only born Englishman who has ever been Pope, ordering the Abbot to render obedience to the Bishop of his diocese. But the other side asked how he had come by these letters, and he had to confess that he had committed the grave irregularity of appealing to Rome without informing his opponents. The King was much more concerned to discover that one of his Bishops had been writing to the Pope without royal permission, which was forbidden by the regulations of William the Conqueror; he flew into such a rage (he was not yet twenty-four) that the case was adjourned until he recovered his temper. In the afternoon the Abbot displayed the foundation charter of his Abbey; but the Bishop contended that a King, a layman, could no more release an Abbot from obedience than he, a Bishop, could free a vassal from allegiance. At this frank exposition of the Guelf point of view the King grew very excited and the court was cleared, each side withdrawing with its supporters; which meant that nearly everyone went out with the Abbot.

The Bishop was displaying great courage. When the King lost his temper he uttered all sorts of extravagant threats, and there was a danger that someone might take him literally and carry out a sentence of hanging or blinding which young Henry would regret when he was calmer. But Hilary was a trained lawyer, with a good case, and he refused to withdraw even after his friends had warned him of the risk.

Thomas the Chancellor made the final speech for the Abbot. Probably he was speaking to a brief, and was thus entitled, as every lawyer is entitled, to advance arguments on behalf of his client which do not represent his own beliefs. For he put the extreme Ghibelline view of the relation between Church and State; the King rules all his subjects, and may alter the powers of Bishops and Abbots as easily as if they were sheriffs and Earls. That was not his opinion in after life, and contemporary clerks thought it a blot on his reputation.

Various explanations are possible. If you think he was a time-server it is easy to say that when he was the King's servant he exalted the royal power and when he was Archbishop he stood out for the rights of his new lord the Pope; but time-servers do not get themselves killed for a principle. Perhaps he was carried away by the joy of battle, in argument against Bishop Hilary the famous Roman lawyer, and snatched at any weapon which might bring him victory. Perhaps he was overcome by patriotic sentiment, wishing to increase the glory of the great memorial to the valour of his ancestors. Perhaps he knew, but did not bother to say, that the Pope had allowed the Conqueror a very free hand, since the King of England was a supporter of the new theories of Church reform, and that if William had asked for Papal confirmation of his exemption he would have got it without question. Perhaps he thought that an arrangement which had stood for eighty years should continue by mere right of prescription. Perhaps he then held views about the power of the Crown which he abandoned in later life, but if so he changed them honestly. In any case, his intervention was decisive; judgment was given for the Abbot of Battle; the Abbey, and the Deanery which succeeded it at the Reformation, remained independent of the Bishop of Chichester until quite recent times.

This was not the first time that Thomas had been opposed to the Bishop of Chichester. As Dean of Hastings he had supported his vicar in his claim to be exempt from episcopal supervision, and had lost. Nor was it to be the last, for Hilary was to become one of his most persistent opponents. Hilary, one of the ablest lawyers in England, was probably unused to losing his cases. Perhaps the memory of his defeat rankled, adding bitterness to the later conflicts of the two men.

Thomas's other principal employment while the peace lasted was an embassy to the King of France. A marriage had been arranged between Henry, the three-year-old son of King Henry, and Margaret, the infant daughter of King Louis VII of France. This was a neat way of settling the question of the Vexin, the disputed borderland between Normandy and the Ile de France; the King of England was determined to have it, and the King of France was too weak to hold it against him; if it was ceded as the dowry of little Margaret honour would be satisfied on both sides.

Even in those days three years was considered too early an age for marriage; but if a girl was destined to wed some particular young man it was thought advisable that they should be brought up together, so that when the time came she would understand how he liked his household to be run. Thomas's mission was to fetch the baby princess to be educated at the English court.

The treaty had been negotiated in advance, and the embassy was a formal visit of courtesy. It was therefore right to make it as splendid as possible, to impress the people of France with the might of the King of England. Henry was skilful at choosing the right minister for any particular mission, and for a mission of splendour he chose his Chancellor. Thomas had plenty of money at his disposal, for besides the income from his own neglected benefices he used at his discretion a vast official revenue; the profits of vacant Bishoprics and Abbeys, and of many fiefs held by minors and unmarried ladies who were wards of the King, were paid direct to the chancery; someone in the office must have kept a record of income and expenditure, but apparently Thomas did not formally account to the King for the way he spent this money in the service of his lord. He now threw himself into the business of organizing the embassy with the skill of a quartermaster and the eye for effect of a theatrical producer.

This was how he entered Paris in the spring of 1158. First came several hundred tall young serving-men in handsome liveries. They marched two by two, and sang in chorus to help them keep in step. Then came twelve magnificent sumpter-horses, the first bearing the portable altar and sacred vessels of the King's private chapel, at whose passing the bystanders must kneel and uncover. Thomas was only a deacon, who cannot say Mass, but there would be plenty of priests among his 'family'. The other eleven pack-horses carried barrels of silver pennies for the living expenses of the mission, and jewellery and goldsmith's work as presents for the French magnates. Each of these sumpter-horses was led by a well-dressed groom, and its load was hidden by costly silks and velvets; as a final touch of fantasy each horse was ridden by a well-dressed monkey. These monkeys were popular pets, but they were expensive and rare: since Africa was unexplored and America undiscovered they could only be brought from India, by the long overland route through the Crusading fiefs of Outremer.

Behind the pack-horses came eight four-wheeled chariots, each drawn by five horses. Such large waggons

were rare in days when most heavy burdens were trans-
ported by water, and they excited as much interest as the
monkeys. The first six carried supplies for the mission,
but the last two were loaded with English ale; some contemporaries say that ale was previously unknown in Paris,
and that the Parisians were thrilled to drink a liquor 'like
wine in colour and equally strong, but clearer and of a
more pleasant flavour'. I should like to think Thomas
introduced beer to Paris, but it had been brewed in
Flanders and the Rhineland from time immemorial and
the odds are he found the town full of frothblowers.

After the waggons rode two hundred knights, the paid
retainers of the Chancellor. (The standard pay of a knight
was eight silver pennies a day in 1100, and twelve in 1200,
because his equipment became every year more complicated and expensive.) Then came a crowd of clerks and
chaplains, and behind them all, which is the place of
honour in an ecclesiastical procession, Thomas the Chancellor, wearing magnificent robes and riding a very fine
war-horse.

The English embassy was splendidly lodged in the
Paris headquarters of the Knights Templars. (This later
became the Temple prison in which Louis XVI and Marie
Antoinette were confined; but in the twelfth century it
was considered very comfortable.) The King of France
saw himself in danger of being overshadowed by this
magnificent subject of the King of England, and to give
the visitors a taste of his majesty he issued orders that anything they fancied in the Paris shops was to be given to
them without argument; but the bill must be sent to the
King of France, and all shopkeepers must refuse English
money.

Perhaps the shopkeepers of Paris had already discovered that Kings pay their debts slowly and reluctantly; perhaps they could not bear to think of all those barrels of English silver going to greedy courtiers instead of to hard-working merchants. Thomas was warned that Louis intended to force the English mission to live on his bounty, and he sent out his purveyors in disguise to buy up all the provisions on the market. He then gave a banquet to the French court, at which we are told one dish of eels cost £100; that is 24,000 silver pennies, the only English coin actually in existence at that time, though money was reckoned in pounds and shillings in accordance with the old English custom of making accountancy as difficult as possible. It sounds an enormous sum to spend on one dish. But Thomas, at this stage of his career, was behaving like a vulgar millionaire, and vulgar millionaires can get through a lot of money at the dinner table.

He remembered with pleasure his days in the Schools. The English Students, when they called on him, pointed out that, like all students everywhere, they were poor and in debt. He gave them money, but the total of their debts was too much even for his lavish purse. To make the future easier for them he gave a splendid banquet to *their creditors*, a charming way of persuading them not to press for payment.

When the time came for the baby princess to set out for her new home in Normandy all Paris agreed that the King of England must be the mightiest potentate in the world, since even his Chancellor lived in such splendour. That was the object of the embassy, and the deliberate waste of the money of a poor country can be defended on grounds of policy. But Thomas had enjoyed himself. He

was exceptionally worldly for a deacon, and old Archbishop Theobald began to regret that he had recommended such a luxurious and secular clerk for the high
office of Chancellor.

On his way back to Normandy Thomas performed his
first military exploit. He captured and put in prison Wido
de la Val, a tiresome robber-knight who plundered the
Seine valley. But he had 200 hired knights to help him,
and he may not have borne arms in person. Yet soon he
was to prove himself a gallant and successful warrior.

CHAPTER FIVE

THOMAS, KNIGHT AND WARRIOR

In 1159 young King Henry was looking round for some field in which to win renown. The idea of naked conquest, at least from a fellow-Christian, was abhorrent to the medieval conscience; if he had tried anything like Frederick the Great's invasion of Silesia, the mere annexation of land because its rightful owner was too weak to guard it, his own knights would have refused to ride with him. Of course such wickedness never entered his mind. But he had already experienced the thrill of riding through conquered cities. As Count of Anjou he was hereditary Seneschal of France, and King Louis, an honourable and rather stupid ruler who did not see that he was increasing the power of a dangerous rival, had commissioned him to bring order to Brittany, ravaged by rival pretenders. The campaign was a mere promenade, in which the King of France joined as an interested spectator; but when the two kings returned to celebrate their triumph in Paris it gradually emerged that the barons of southern Brittany had become the vassals of the Duke of Normandy. He had already increased the fiefs he had inherited from his ancestors; in what direction should he lead his army for the next campaigning season?

The Count of Toulouse was one of the six lay Peers of

France, as great a lord as the Duke of Normandy; of course he did homage directly to the King. But ancient records showed that at one time Toulouse had been subordinate to Aquitaine, and when Henry demanded homage he could claim that he was merely reviving long-forgotten rights. The Count refused, and Henry mustered his forces for bitter full-scale war.

He did not wish to employ the feudal levy of England. Anglo-Norman knights wore old-fashioned equipment, and they were less skilled in the joust than Frenchmen, who had plenty of practice in the new tournaments, forbidden in England as dangerous to the peace. In any case, wars were increasingly fought by professional soldiers, and he could hire soldiers in Aquitaine more cheaply than he could transport his vassals, with their horses and followers, all the way from Southampton. But he needed money, and accordingly he taxed his towns and serfs, which were his absolutely and could not argue about the sum demanded; he then came to a friendly arrangement with his free vassals by which they paid 'scutage' or shield-money. They might of course stand out for their right of fighting instead of paying, but on active service there would be ways of making them wish they had stayed at home.

The question arose whether the lands of the Church were liable for scutage. It was a new question, previously undecided, because a general scutage instead of armed service was a new expedient. Bishops and Abbots held land by knight-service, and would have been liable to send knights if knights had been demanded; but in the past they had normally been excused scutage. That is not to say they were excused taxation; the Pope taxed them heavily, both to pay for his court and for the strengthening of the Crusading fortresses of Outremer; and the revenues of all vacant Bishoprics and Abbeys went automatically to the King. Because rich churches usually possessed vessels of gold and silver the King was in the habit of seizing their valuables in an emergency, promising to repay the debt when he could afford it. The twelfth-century Church contributed its share to the obligations of society.

The Bishops and Abbots, assembled in council, were inclined to resist the King's new demand; if they had refused unanimously it is hard to see what he could have done; for in the Middle Ages the taxation of free men always needed their consent. But Thomas the Chancellor argued them into consenting, partly by threats of what would happen if they displeased the King, partly because they knew he had been the trusted clerk of the Archbishop and his opinion carried weight as that of a trained lawyer of Roman inclinations. The Bishops and Abbots paid up; yet afterwards they blamed Thomas as a renegade, a turncoat who had been false to his Order.

Throughout his life Thomas was extremely clumsy in his handling of public opinion. He was a good man of affairs who could give sensible orders, but he usually miscalculated the effect of his actions on the ordinary man in the street. It seems that he hardly considered the rights of the question, so anxious was he to raise money for the first important campaign of his adored master and friend. He was surprised that any vassal should make difficulties when the King proposed to enforce his rights over those faithless rebels of Toulouse. In later days he admitted, wearily, that he might have been mistaken in a technical question of law, but he never understood why people made such a fuss about it.

Thomas had by this time assumed the position of Henry's elder brother, who feels that his junior cannot carry out any undertaking without his presence and advice. Henry could never win a war unless his Chancellor was there to keep him out of trouble. Therefore, when the army rode eastward from Aquitaine, Thomas, who was forty years old and had once assisted at the capture of a robber-knight, led a large contingent for whose pay he had made himself responsible. How much of the money he spent was the income of the chancery, and therefore the King's, and how much came from his own benefices and was his to give, we cannot say; probably Thomas could not say either.

The Count dared not meet Henry's enormous army in the field, and shut himself up in the strong fortress of Toulouse; he also took the obvious step of appealing to his liege-lord for assistance, which is what liege-lords are for. King Louis also could not face Henry's army, but he always fulfilled the feudal duties of his position, and he slipped into the besieged town to afford his vassal moral support. Henry's army lay before Toulouse from June to November, and then retired for lack of provisions; an assault would probably have carried the walls, but no assault was attempted.

The reason for this lack of enterprise was a point of feudal ethics. Henry, as Duke of Normandy and Aquitaine, had sworn liege homage to Louis, and it would be felony to assault a town which sheltered his lord. Thomas could not see the force of the argument, and continually urged Henry to capture the place; but Thomas was a clerk, brought up in the mercantile atmosphere of London, and he could not pick his way through the intricate maze of feudal rights as surely as a young warrior who had governed Normandy at the age of seventeen. Henry was a more or less absolute King of England, as successor to the Conqueror; but he held Normandy, Aquitaine and Anjou only because his vassals had sworn fealty; if he set them the example of breaking his feudal oath they would not keep their faith with him. The war with Toulouse was a just war, between two equal tenants-in-chief of the King of France; the arrival of King Louis turned Henry's invasion into a rebellion.

A quibble was discovered by which the war might continue; Thomas had never sworn allegiance to anyone except the King of England, and he might fight the King of France with a clear conscience. After Henry retired the Chancellor remained in command of his own troops and certain reinforcements, with the Earl of Essex as military adviser. An energetic and spirited commander, though a novice, may accomplish much on his first campaign, and Thomas captured the city of Cahors and several strong castles. We are told that he led the escalade in full mail, displaying great courage and prowess. It is not at all surprising; he was by descent a Norman warrior, and to him warfare came naturally. Later his enemies pointed out that he had taken the sword, and therefore he perished by the sword; but that saying of Our Lord has always seemed to me a promise, not a threat; surely there is no better way of dying.

In the winter the war moved north to the Vexin, the disputed borderland which Louis regretted having ceded as his daughter's dowry. Henry might lawfully defend his own land even against his liege-lord, and he held the field against the King of France. In those days campaigns turned on the siege and defence of castles, and pitched battles were very rare; but there was constant skirmishing at the outposts, and famous champions would challenge any knight on the other side to meet them in the joust. When Engelram de Trie, a famous French hero, challenged the Normans in this way Thomas, Chancellor and deacon, rode against him; it was Engelram who was unseated, and Thomas led back his warhorse as a trophy, as though the joust had been a tournament. A very good warrior was lost when that tall eager Norman took orders.

In this campaign Thomas hired, from his jumble of incomes, 700 knights, 1,200 horsemen of lesser rank, and 4,000 foot, and we are told his contingent was the most efficient in Henry's army. He was perfectly happy, doing well an important job which also interested and amused him, and winning the respect of knights and barons, which he probably valued more highly than the good opinion of clerks.

But the wars of the twelfth century, so lightly begun, could be easily ended. In November a truce was arranged, which led to a permanent peace in May 1160. In accordance with the diplomatic practice of the time the treaty did not mention Toulouse or the Vexin; in fact nothing in dispute was settled, and the war could begin again when either party felt inclined.

The Chancellor had not previously been one of the high officers of state; he was the King's private secretary rather than a responsible minister. But Thomas was so much in his master's confidence, and had such energy and drive, that he became almost Henry's colleague in the

King Henry II

From his first Great Seal, in use 1155–8. This is the Seal that Thomas
used as Chancellor. The King must have approved the design, and it
is probably reasonably accurate, for a mediaeval portrait

administration of his enormous dominions. The Chancellor was entitled by custom to a daily wage of five shillings (five times the pay of a knight), and to a generous ration of food, wine and candles from the officials of the household. That shows that he normally lodged in the King's hall, with the other retainers. Thomas set up a household of his own, and a very splendid one. In fact the King complained, though he made a joke of it, that those of his visitors who appreciated good food made a practice of dining with the Chancellor, so that he never saw them at meal-times. Seven-year-old Henry, the King's son and heir, was sent to live with the Chancellor, in accordance with the belief of the Middle Ages that a boy's own parents would not beat him enough to teach him good manners. Naturally every fashionable baron wished to send his son to the household which had been entrusted with the education of the heir to the throne, and a crowd of noble pages waited on Thomas. I have already mentioned the magnificence of his dress. Even in the more useful branches of administration he was better supplied than the King. Henry was continually crossing between Normandy and England, but he had only one private yacht; Thomas had six, each bigger than the King's, and Henry was frequently compelled to borrow them as a favour when he wished to move court and baggage across the Channel.

Thomas was of course very busy, but he amused himself when he had the time. His favourite outdoor pastime was hawking, which can be fitted into an odd hour or two and does not take all day like finding and running down a stag. Indoors he was fond of chess. That is nowadays a serious intellectual pursuit, eminently suitable for deacons. But before playing-cards had been invented many laymen played chess quickly and badly, purely as a gamble, and the villain losing more than he can afford and trying to brain the hero with the chess-board is one of the stock incidents of medieval romance; it was considered a fast dissipation, rather like poker at the present time.

Thomas even had the bits of his horses made of silver, which shows the vulgar streak in the son of the London merchant; a bit made of silver would be a very bad bit, too soft and tasting horrible in the horse's mouth; and it would not even look so smart as properly burnished steel.

He seemed to be in everything the willing and even obsequious servant of the King; but about this time a minor incident showed he still had certain principles. Henry had consented to a marriage between Philip Count of Flanders and Mary the daughter of King Stephen. But Mary had taken vows as a nun, and was actually Abbess of Barking. The marriage took place, against all the rules of the Church; probably most of the King's advisers were glad to see a daughter of old King Stephen leave the country, for she might have been a figurehead for rebellion; but Thomas spoke against it so strongly that the Count of Flanders swore vengeance. It is worth remembering that in future it would be unsafe for him to land unprotected in Flanders.

Then old Archbishop Theobald grew very ill, and felt he had not much longer to live. For some time he had been worried to see his favourite clerk leading such an unclerical and dissipated life. He sent a message asking Thomas to visit him at Canterbury; but Thomas was in Normandy with the King, much too busy to visit old gentlemen on their sick-beds. He did not send a definite refusal, but neither did he go to Canterbury. Theobald fretted, and it became one of those obsessions which make invalids so difficult to deal with. He sent message after message beseeching Thomas to come, and at last went so far as to threaten him with excommunication for disobeying the orders of his canonical superior. But it is possible this was only a joke; the letter remains, but it is not easy to interpret the spirit in which these ancient letters were written. In any case, though Theobald was Metropolitan, that did not give him the right to order one of the King's servants to drop his work and sail from Normandy to England. At last, in April 1161, Theobald died, without seeing Thomas. But we must remember that Thomas was in fact employed in important and responsible work.

CHAPTER SIX

ARCHBISHOP OF CANTERBURY

For the first time since 1138, more than twenty years, the Archbishopric of Canterbury was vacant. It was the most important post in the kingdom, and the King was in no hurry to fill it. During vacancy its revenues were paid to the Crown, which was another reason for Henry to take his time; London and Worcester were also vacant, and it so happened that these revenues were paid through the chancery, and Thomas had the handling of them. Many people thought he encouraged the King to leave Bishoprics vacant, to spend the proceeds on his own extravagant household, where he had now taken to laying clean rushes on the floor every day, and even sometimes taking up the dirty ones.

Sooner or later the King must see to it that these Bishoprics were filled; otherwise the Pope would take action. But the question of the appointment of Bishops was now in a thorough tangle, and he could keep Rome quiet for years by making an opening move and then allowing a long interval for reflection.

In the Primitive Church the successors of the Apostles were chosen by the whole of their flock; but Christians were then a small minority, able to assemble in one room. Even after Constantine had changed the religion of most of his subjects Bishops were sometimes chosen by a mass-meeting of the faithful; the adjutant of the Imperial Guard in Milan must have been rather annoyed when his orderly officer was chosen because he happened to walk past the meeting while inspecting his sentries (yet Ambrose became a great Bishop and a Saint). Later the election was confined to the clergy of the Diocese, and by the twelfth century it had become the privilege of the canons of the Cathedral Church, as it still is. In England, the place of the Cathedral Clergy was taken, in some eight or nine cathedrals, by monks. The monks of Christchurch, Canterbury chose the clerk who, after due consecration, would become Metropolitan.

Yet monks who never left Canterbury and saw very little of the world were unfitted to choose the most important subject of the King. On some of the occasions when they were allowed to choose freely they fixed on someone quite unsuitable. Pressure was brought to bear on them to indicate a suitable candidate.

The man who could bring most pressure was obviously the Pope. If the monks neglected to elect at all he might fill the vacancy without consulting anyone; also if a Bishop died at his court he had the perquisite of conferring the vacant See without further formality. Bishop Hilary of Chichester had been appointed in this way. Yet the Pope often thought more of finding an income for some useful member of his Curia than of the needs of the vacant Diocese; nobody wanted the appointment to lapse to Rome, least of all the monks of Christ Church who would be deprived of the privilege of election.

The Bishops of the Province claimed to speak at the election; they might not vote, but they were intimately concerned with the personality of their new Metropolitan, and they could propose a candidate. If they were unanimous, or nearly so, their view would carry great weight with the monks.

But the man who had the deciding voice, in practice though not in theory, was the King. Nowadays the Prime Minister, in the Queen's name, orders a Cathedral chapter to elect a named individual, and the canons would face imprisonment if they disobeyed. (Yet if they were willing to go to prison the candidate would not be Bishop; election is still essential.) At that time no election might be held until the King had given permission, and he might stipulate that it be held in his presence. He could tell the monks whom to elect; though of course they might disobey him and brave the undefined but menacing consequences. In later life Henry indicated his wishes pretty brusquely; in 1173 he wrote 'to his faithful monks of the church of Winchester, greeting:—I order you to hold free election, but nevertheless I forbid you to elect anyone except Richard my clerk, archdeacon of Poictiers.' But in 1161 he was younger, his temper was under better control, and he was a little more careful of the forms of ecclesiastical liberty.

The reason why the King took such an interest was that every Bishop was also a powerful baron; the Bishop of Durham defended the Border against the Scots (in 1745 he still led the militia of Durham against the Jacobites); the Bishop of Winchester had more knights in his service than any Earl; and the Archbishop of Canterbury was the first subject of the realm, the traditional mediator between King and people. It was his duty to rebuke the King if his rule became tyrannous; Anselm had dared to rebuke William Rufus, who heard him with surprisingly good grace. The holders of such great baronies must be loyal subjects, and in later times King John had a legitimate grievance when a Scot was chosen Bishop of Hereford while he was actually waging war with Scotland. In modern eyes it seems that the obvious solution would have been to give the baronies to laymen, and to choose Bishops for their spiritual qualifications. But to take land from the Church would have been considered sacrilege. We must remember that most of it had not been given by the crown, but by pious barons and knights; their descendants would rebel if they saw the endowments of their ancestors confiscated to secular uses.

These baronies had already been the source of an obstinate contest between Pope and King; the King said that all barons must swear homage, the Pope said it was simony for a Bishop to swear homage to a layman. On the Continent this led to long wars between Pope and Emperor, but in England the King had won easily, so easily that he allowed the Church to save appearances by a typically English compromise. The Bishop-elect swore homage before he was consecrated. Thus Bishops did not swear homage, but every Bishop was a man who had already sworn, and homage endured for life.

For a year Canterbury remained vacant, while the Pope, the King, and the Bishops conferred unofficially, trying to find a candidate acceptable to all interests. If what was needed was a competent churchman, of holy life and unblemished loyalty to the King, a gentleman of good birth who had already proved himself a good Bishop, there was no need to look far. Gilbert Foliot, Bishop of Hereford, was a former protégé of Theobald, of good birth and kin to all the great Marcher houses;

he was cousin to the Clares and his brother was Abbot of Evesham. In early life he had entered the great monastery of Cluny, the holiest monastery in Christendom; more than ten years ago the Pope had appointed him to Hereford; and he ruled his See so efficiently, and with such zeal for religion, that the King had wished him to administer the vacant See of London. But he very honestly refused this interesting and important post, because he feared that if he accepted London would never be filled, and the King would enjoy its revenue while the work was done at Hereford's expense. His friends took it for granted that he would be the next Archbishop.

But the King had a brain-wave. His faithful friend Thomas got through all the work of the chancery, and still found plenty of time for hawking and feasting. He was technically a clerk though he lived like a layman, and from his days as archdeacon he knew the routine of a Bishopric. If he were Archbishop as well as Chancellor he would be supreme over both branches of the administration, and there would be no danger of a conflict between Church and State. There were recent precedents for the appointment. The Emperor employed as Chancellor in Germany the Archbishop of Mainz, and as Chancellor in Italy the Archbishop of Cologne; no one minded, and it proved that a Chancellor could be Archbishop in his spare time. For of course Henry took it for granted that the chancery would come first. All the same, such an arrangement was a novelty in England, and the King allowed the news of his intention to leak out unofficially, to see how it was received.

The Pope at once fell in with the idea; what Rome looked for in Archbishops was a knowledge of Canon

Law, and Thomas was remembered as a learned lawyer; apart from that the busier he was with secular affairs the better; there was no room for a forceful personality between the Curia and the Diocesan Bishops. Cardinal Henry of Pisa, the Papal envoy at Henry's court, supported the appointment. But in the English Church there was dismay. Just when they had all made up their minds to propose Gilbert of Hereford, such an excellent candidate, the King was going to embezzle the income of the richest Diocese in the realm for the benefit of a royal clerk, who in any dispute would take the King's side. The Church would be without a head. The English Bishops knew Thomas personally, and disliked what they knew. Rome might consider him a distinguished lawyer, but since last he had visited the Curia he had become a luxurious baron, leading seven hundred knights in the field and jousting against French champions; and there was the scandal of his dress and his costly dinners.

But they realized that Henry was in earnest, and would have his way. The only remedy that remained was to persuade Thomas to alter his manner of living. John of Salisbury, his old friend and colleague, who happened to have business at court, called on the Chancellor, and found him playing chess at a table littered with gold and silver, the stakes and the side-bets; he was dressed like a baron and his long embroidered sleeves, the latest fashion from Paris, swept the floor. John reminded him that he was a deacon, at present enjoying the revenues of London, Worcester and Canterbury, and probably soon to be Archbishop. Couldn't he dress more soberly, and give up all this gambling? Thomas returned a polite answer, but he did not mend his ways.

In fact he was passing through a great crisis. He had lived at close quarters with a holy Archbishop of Canterbury and he knew the duties of the position. His will was always in complete control of his body; he never dismounted because he was saddle-sore, or broke the rules of fasting because he was hungry or thirsty, or rested because he was tired; with all his vulgar love of splendour he was indifferent to comfort. He did not fear death, which is luckily a common virtue; but he was also quite unmoved by browbeating and abuse from his superiors, which is much more rare; above all he valued his reputation in the eyes of the world. He had been a brave knight, a successful cavalry leader, a competent lawyer, and an exceptionally able Chancellor. If he became Archbishop he knew that his fierce energy and determination would make him a good Archbishop, but he also knew that a good Archbishop would be forced to quarrel with the King; and Henry was the only friend in all the world whom he loved as a man.

He tried to refuse the great promotion. At Falaise in the spring of 1162 the King summoned him into his presence and begged him to accept. Thomas looked down at his gorgeous robes and tried to pass off his answer as a joke. 'What a religious and saintly man you wish to place in that holy Bishopric, over so famous a monastery!' he said. 'If it were to happen the love you now bear me would turn to bitter hatred. For you would require of me many things which I could not bear quietly.' That was fair warning, but Henry disregarded it. The Cardinal of Pisa added his entreaties, and finally Thomas accepted, against his better judgement.

When all had been arranged Henry sent to the monks

of Christ Church his permission to elect. Thomas crossed the Channel and rode to London, but Henry remained as usual in Normandy; little Henry, aged seven, was in London, and could give the ceremonial royal assent to the choice of the electors.

Of course there was no doubt about the result. The monks had been persuaded, and the Bishops had made up their minds to agree with a good grace, since very soon this King's clerk would be their superior. Only Gilbert of Hereford, when he saw this worldling actually elected to the position which he knew himself so well fitted to hold, lost his temper and made a scene. But he had no vote, and the election remained unanimous. There was a good deal of sympathy for Gilbert; he was not especially ambitious, but he had been led to expect promotion and disappointed at the last minute. We must remember that it was the custom of the age for great men to display their feelings on ceremonial occasions, instead of wearing a fixed smile of goodwill and publishing their memoirs afterwards.

As soon as he was elected, but while in religion he was still no more than a deacon, Thomas swore homage to little Henry, who never reigned and is not numbered among the Henrys; it will be convenient to refer to him in future as the Young King, his appellation while he lived. That should have ended the ceremony, but before the gathering could disperse Henry of Winchester, the senior Bishop, suggested in the name of all his colleagues that Thomas should receive a formal release from any debts or services he owed the King. Little Henry murmured some formula, and Thomas might proceed to consecration unhampered by worldly ties. Later Thomas and his supporters attached great importance to this release, holding that it debarred the King from ever demanding the accounts of the chancery; but when it was made he was still Chancellor, and as far as anyone knew he intended to remain in office. It cannot have meant that the Chancellor need not keep accounts; probably it meant nothing in particular, except that he had the King's goodwill.

The next stage after election was consecration. Thomas rode in state to Canterbury, where all the Bishops of his Province assembled for the Feast of Pentecost. On the Saturday after Pentecost he was ordained priest, and on Sunday the 3rd of June 1162 he was consecrated by the Bishop of Winchester, who was the senior Bishop in England and also the most important socially, since he was the brother of the late King Stephen. Thomas immediately said his first Mass in the chapel of the Holy Trinity behind the high altar of the Cathedral, and in memory of this occasion the Feast of the Trinity, which had been observed by the Saxons, and the Normans had abolished, was restored to the English Calendar.

Thomas was now a Bishop; there was one more formality before he could exercise authority over his suffragans; he must receive the pallium, the white halter-like vestment which the Pope bestows on all Metropolitans as a sign that they possess some of his delegated authority. Many Archbishops visited the Pope to receive it, but Thomas was very busy and Alexander III was anxious to be helpful; the Emperor had driven him from Rome and he was staying at Montpellier in France; he sent the pallium to Canterbury, where it arrived on the 10th of August. To show his reverence for Papal authority Thomas walked barefoot to meet it, and when it had been hung round his neck he was Archbishop, Papal Legate with authority in the Province of York, first subject of the realm; and incidentally Chancellor as well.

But almost at once he resigned the chancery, to the King's great annoyance. In any case he could not have performed its duties, for he insisted on staying in Canterbury to carry out the routine of his new office. It has been said of him that he was not naturally a good man, but that he first learned what a saint was expected to do and then went and did it. That was said as a slur on his character, but to me it seems the highest praise; Anselm was holy by nature and earned sanctity by following his own inclinations; but Thomas had to discipline his instincts with the watchfulness and self-control of a sentinel on a dangerous post.

He had entered a new world, and though he was anxious to comply with its customs he began by making mistakes. As Archbishop he was *ex officio* Abbot of Christ Church, and he had not lived among monks since he left school at Merton. He attended as many of the monastic offices as he could, especially Matins at midnight; he could not attend them all, for a monk spends eight hours a day in choir. But it did not occur to him to alter his secular dress, and he stood out among the black-robed Benedictines who clustered round flickering candles in the dark empty Cathedral. When it was pointed out to him that he was distracting the monks from their prayers he adopted the black gown and white surplice of the Augustinians of Merton, which he had worn as a schoolboy; though he continued to wear his gay clothes underneath, using the gown as an overcoat against the chill of the gaunt Cathedral.

In the same way he continued his magnificent dinners, though his cross-bearer read from a holy book in the place of the musicians and jongleurs who had entertained the Chancellor. His companions at table were all monks or clerks, though there was another table for laymen, where they could tell one another lay stories without hearing the pious reading. On one occasion a boorish monk rebuked him for eating pheasant, the supreme delicacy of the twelfth-century table. He replied that he ate less of his pheasant than the monk ate of his porridge, and that gluttony was eating too much, not eating delicate food. That may be a quibble, but at least he had kept his temper when he might excusably have been angry.

All this may have been a striving for effect, nothing more than willingness to please public opinion (though willingness to please public opinion can be the source of good actions). His hair shirt is a different matter. This he wore under his fine linen shirt, a secret from all but his valet; his valet knew because he washed it, and Thomas was fastidious in cleanliness; after his death two clean hair shirts were found among his effects, besides the one he was wearing. He can only have worn it as a penance between himself and God; apparently he knew that he lived too softly, and felt guilty about it; but he could not abandon his splendour.

We have an account of his daily life at Canterbury, which shows what strenuous efforts he made to play his part. He rose at midnight to attend Matins, then washed the feet of twelve poor men and gave them a meal with his own hands. Then he went back to bed; but he rose at dawn, and read the Bible with Herbert of Bosham, his chaplain. At 9 he said Mass, always a very short Mass with as few Collects as possible; he had never said Mass until he was forty-three, and he could not fix his attention on the ceremony if it continued too long. After breakfast he would read and answer his letters, sticking to his desk until dinner-time soon after midday; in the afternoon he took a siesta, then rode out for exercise, wearing his stole in case he should have an opportunity to administer Confirmation. There were no more than seventeen Bishops in England, and Confirmation was always a problem; casual wayfarers would accost any Bishop, or a crowd would wait by appointment at some crossroads; the ceremony was always held in the open air. But his contemporaries noted that Thomas dismounted to confirm, such was his reverence for the Sacrament; unlike some other Bishops who pushed their horses through the throng, tapping every head they could reach. After his ride he would eat a light supper and go to bed early, in readiness for Matins at midnight.

In 1162 King Henry came to England for Christmas, and Thomas met him at Southampton. The courtiers were relieved to see they were still excellent friends, though Henry was annoyed with Thomas for resigning the chancery. The King visited Canterbury for Palm Sunday 1163, and graciously walked with the Archbishop in the customary procession. But it was thought a bad omen that all the decorations in the streets were blown down during the previous night. Perhaps these Normans were not yet reconciled to the usual fate of open-air festivities in England.

In May Alexander III held a Council to excommunicate the Antipope who had turned him out of Rome. The King of England was the most important follower of the rightful Pope, and the Council was held in his city of Tours (part of his Angevin inheritance), as a compliment to him. Thomas attended, with most of the English Bishops; he was invited to preach on Trinity Sunday, roughly a year after his consecration, and refused, as already stated; his diffidence is understandable, for he was nearly forty-five and had not yet been ordained for a whole year. This Council was purely a demonstration, to show the world that the Kings of France and England supported the rightful Pope, and it made no important decisions.

The first year of Thomas's Archbishopric had passed peacefully, though since the King spent most of his time in France and Thomas in England the two friends were no longer so intimate. But now the troubles began. The King wished his illegitimate brother William to marry the widow of Stephen's son, who was Countess of Warenne in her own right. But they were cousins, and a dispensation was needed. Thomas refused it, though these favours were more or less taken for granted. We do not know why he refused, perhaps merely to show his independence; but perhaps Isabel de Warenne was unwilling.

Then there was a difference about money, a subject very close to Henry's heart. At Woodstock in July the King proposed to his barons that a small tax called the Sheriff's Aid should in future be paid to the Exchequer, instead of to the sheriffs' private purse. This tax was what the Americans call a 'racket'; every landowner subscribed, and in return the sheriff did not harass him by collecting obsolete dues of a pig here and a dozen eggs there, which had been paid to the Saxon Kings. The barons saw at once that if this tax went to the Exchequer they would have to raise another subscription to pacify the sheriff, for all sheriffs expected to grow rich in a few years, and paid the King heavily for their appointments; the Archbishop of Canterbury led the opposition, and the King gave way.

About this time King Henry intervened personally in one of the frequent disputes over the rival jurisdiction of Church courts and King's courts. One Philip de Brois, a canon of Bedford, was accused of the murder of a layman; in accordance with Church law he was charged with this crime in the court of the Bishop of Lincoln, and acquitted. But public opinion was convinced that he was in fact a murderer, and the sheriff brought him before the King's Justice in Eyre who was sitting at Dunstable. Philip refused to plead, as he was entitled to do; but he then put himself in the wrong by making offensive remarks about the judge, and by implication about the King who had commissioned him. Henry was very angry when he heard of it, and demanded that the Archbishop should force the canon to stand to trial in the lay court. This Thomas would not grant, for it would be yielding a vital principle; but he did not approve of canons who committed murder, and he called up the suit for another trial before his own court in Canterbury; there seem to have been no particular grounds for appeal, but nobody minded, for in the twelfth century appealing was always very easy. In this second trial Philip was again acquitted of murder, but he was then charged with contempt of court for his insolence to the King's judge at Dunstable. For this offence he was punished very heavily; he was sentenced to be flogged, and to forfeit two years' income from his canonry. Henry now went about saying that the Archbishop allowed clerks to murder laymen with impunity; but since Philip was twice tried and twice acquitted a reasonable explanation would be that someone else had done the murder. Certainly the Archbishop's court had shown itself willing to protect the dignity of the King's judges by a penalty which would ensure that accused clerks minded their manners in future.

Thomas also infringed the customs of William the Conqueror by excommunicating a tenant-in-chief without first consulting the King. William de Eynsford claimed an advowson which belonged to the See of Canterbury, and forcibly intruded his candidate when he lost his case. He merited excommunication, but since no Christian might have any dealings with an excommunicate he was now incapable of joining the King's army; or if he did everyone else ought to leave it. The King had a legitimate grievance, though Thomas had kept the letter of Canon Law. By autumn Henry thought it was time to bring his Archbishop to heel.

A more or less routine Council was held at Westminster in October 1163; the agenda was mainly ecclesiastical, dealing with little but the exemption of the Abbey of St. Albans from episcopal control and the perennial dispute about the powers of the Archbishop of York. But King Henry came in person, and suddenly announced that all the Bishops present must swear immediately to observe the ancient customs of the realm. He did not define these ancient customs, and they needed definition; for William the Conqueror had been more absolute than any of his successors, Rufus had done many things which were now regarded as abuses, and Stephen had allowed the Church a great deal of liberty. If Henry might quote as a binding precedent anything that had been done by any previous King of England he would be complete master of the Church.

The Bishops were taken by surprise, but there was a well-known formula which could be used to dodge almost any issue. Thomas swore to observe the customs 'saving the rights of his order', and his suffragans followed his example; except Hilary of Chichester, who swore 'in good faith'. No one knew what he meant by it, but it was felt that he was letting down the side. The King retired in one of his famous rages, and next morning it was discovered that he had ridden away, leaving no address. But he had made some extremely unpleasant threats before he left, and the Bishops were worried and frightened.

That was exactly what Henry wanted. He knew he could not overcome a united Church of England, but he also knew that three Bishops disliked their leader, and he counted on time to split their ranks. The three were Hilary of Chichester, who had never forgiven his defeat over Battle Abbey, Gilbert Foliot now Bishop of London, who had been disappointed of the Archbishopric, and Roger of York, who despised 'Bailhache' and perpetually disputed the supremacy of Canterbury. Then the Pope, who was living at Sens, unusually handy for messengers from England, was anxious to avoid a quarrel with King Henry, on whose support he depended now that Italy and Germany were under the sway of the Antipope. He would be reluctant to support the Archbishop against the Crown.

Since the alleged customs had never been defined no one knew exactly what the dispute was about, but everyone concerned with international affairs accused Thomas of upsetting the unity of the Papalist party by picking an unnecessary quarrel. Alexander sent a very influential envoy, Robert of Melun, Thomas's old tutor in Paris and soon to be Bishop of Hereford; the Bishop of Lisieux in Normandy also intervened, and various distinguished French Abbots and theologians passed to and fro as intermediaries. Thomas was in a genuine dilemma; his position was roughly that he would carry out the wishes of the King in any concrete case, so long as the King did not press him too hard; but he would not make a public promise which would bind all succeeding Archbishops of Canterbury; in fact he would not give the King a blank cheque.

In the end he was overborne; he persuaded himself that obedience to the Pope came before the preservation of the liberties of the Church, and that the Pope had ordered him to swear; though the Pope maintained afterwards that he had *advised* the Archbishop to come to terms with the King, but had never *ordered* him to swear to the customs. About Christmas he sought out the King at Woodstock and promised that next time he was asked in public he would give a satisfactory answer. Perhaps he tried to arrange some compromise at the same time; but this was a private interview, and even his supporters were left in ignorance that he had given way.

CHAPTER SEVEN

CLARENDON

In January 1164 the King held a Council at Clarendon. This was not mainly for Bishops, like the meeting at Westminster; all barons had been summoned and in theory any tenant-in-chief might come without summons; the barons of course brought their household knights, and the lay warriors greatly outnumbered the clerks.

Clarendon was not a castle. It had been built as a hunting-lodge, but Henry visited it frequently, and room had been added to room until it could lodge a large number of guests. Probably most of the visitors brought tents as well; we know that in the next century when Henry III visited Westminster, his largest palace, the first thing the servants did was to pitch the tents. Perhaps the choice of an unfortified dwelling was a deliberate gesture of peace; even if the Bishops quarrelled with the King they might ride home safely, without being stopped by the sentry on the gate.

The Bishops were nervous, but determined to stand firm. Even those who disliked Thomas had made up their minds to back him, at least until they saw what reprisals the King would threaten; for in the twelfth century the rights of his order were very dear even to a royalist clerk.

But the King began by raising a matter which had very little to do with the rights of Bishops; the question of the trial and punishment of clerks accused of felony, that is of grave crimes against the peace, especially homicide and treason. It is essential, to understand the quarrel which followed, to realize that both parties were trying to alter the law, though both parties denied it. Henry had succeeded to the throne as the heir of King Stephen, in accordance with the terms of the Treaty of Winchester; King Stephen was recognized in every official document as having been rightful King of England. But King Henry, at the back of his mind, thought of Stephen as an unlawful usurper; he dared not say so openly, for it would have called his own title into question, but he was inclined to disregard any precedent from the reign of his immediate predecessor, and claim that the true Law of England (which of course was unalterable and eternal) was to be found in the practice of King Henry I, his maternal grandfather.

But in fact the practice of administration, though not the Law of the land, had changed considerably in the last thirty years. The idea that all clerks, even those in the lowest of minor orders, were members of the great international commonwealth of the clerical estate, not to be judged by any lay court, was a new conception. It had been in the air when William the Conqueror was crowned at Westminster, and in fact he had favoured it by setting up a special court for the Bishops whom he had found sitting in judgment as colleagues of the sheriffs. But in no realm in Christendom was the new claim of the Church completely acknowledged. Pope Gregory VII had complained when the Conqueror imprisoned the Bishop of

Bayeux, and William had answered by sending to Rome the mail-shirt in which the warlike rebel had been captured, with the terse quotation (addressed to Jacob in the Bible), 'Is this thy son's coat?' But in most countries some friendly compromise was reached. The right of free communication with the Pope had also been hindered, or granted grudgingly, by the Conqueror, though King Stephen had allowed it when he found himself in need of the Church's support; that gave it a standing of thirty years, quite long enough to found a custom.

We must remember that a medieval criminal court did not attempt to discover the truth about an unsolved crime. If a criminal was taken in the act he was held in custody until the King's judge came to the district, and then brought before him for the formality of sentence; if he was a thief who had been caught with his booty he might be brought into court with the stolen goods strapped to him, to prove his guilt. The judge then declared the convict to be in the King's mercy, and the King might inflict any punishment he chose on one who had broken the Law and so put himself outside its protection. Thus William the Conqueror could substitute blinding for hanging, and Rufus reintroduce capital punishment, without altering the unalterable Law of England. But if the prisoner was merely suspected by the opinion of the countryside the court proceeded to trial. No evidence was heard, and no inquiries were made; instead the culprit must produce twelve men of his own social standing who were willing to swear he was innocent, in which case he was immediately acquitted. Or, if he could not persuade his friends to swear to his innocence, for in the twelfth century there was a genuine and widespread fear of the spiritual consequences of perjury, he might try his luck with the Ordeal, grasping hot iron to see whether it burned him or jumping into a pond to see whether he floated or sank. (Surviving records show that about half those who undertook the Ordeal satisfied the examiners; either miracles were very common in those days or the priest who supervised the heating of the iron could be got at.)

The important thing, from Henry's point of view, was that the chattels of a felon went to the King, and his land to his lord (who was often the King). If he was acquitted his accusers would be in mercy for deceiving the court, and the judge might inflict a money penalty as an 'amercement'. Some figures may be useful, though they date from the next generation; at the Gloucester Assizes of 1221 the judges were faced with 330 charges of homicide; for these 15 murderers were executed, and 100 fugitives outlawed. Thus 215 murders were left unsolved and unavenged. *But* the chattels of the guilty, and the amercement of the unsuccessful accusers, the suitors, and in general everyone connected with the Assize, brought in the large sum of £430. A famous lawyer of those days laid it down that 'Justice is a great source of income', and we see what he meant.

The ecclesiastical courts were just as incompetent at finding out the truth, though they preferred oath-swearing to the Ordeal; in fact they clung to it long after the secular courts had begun to hear evidence, and in the fourteenth century the burgesses of London decreed that professional oath-swearers who earned a living by hanging round the court of the archdeacon and swearing to the innocence of total strangers were ineligible to serve on a London jury. If a clerk was unlucky enough, or truthful enough, to be convicted by this process, the worst that could happen to him was to be deprived of his orders; he was then a layman, in danger of the King's justice the next time he committed a felony, but in the meantime nobody got any chattels or any amercement. Since there were a great many clerks in minor orders, living like laymen and frequently committing felonies, the King's income was seriously diminished.

Henry proposed that after a clerk had been found guilty in the Church court, and stripped of his orders so that he was now a layman, he should be sent to the King's judge to receive sentence of death (there would be no need for another trial). Then the King would get his chattels.

Henry said that this was the ancient custom of the realm, in particular the custom of his grandfather Henry I. It had never been the custom, though in the eleventh century it had been common for felonious clerks to be *first* found guilty in the King's court, and then handed over to the Church court for punishment; even then the Bishop's official must be on the alert; the King's judge resented this handing over, and unless the official was present to receive the prisoner when sentence was passed the hanging would follow immediately. Bishops had complained that their clerks were sometimes hanged hurriedly in the dinner-hour while no one was looking.

Thomas was making a new claim when he held that clerks might only be tried and punished by ecclesiastical courts, even for crimes which would have brought death to a layman. But Henry was making a new claim when he ordered that all guilty clerks should be sentenced in the royal courts. Thomas pointed out that not only was it an alteration of the unalterable Law of England, it was unjust in itself, since it entailed two punishments for one offence. In his view the deprivation of orders was a very severe punishment, quite enough to inflict even for murder.

The lay barons were strongly in favour of a scheme which would increase the King's income; less would be demanded from them. But all the Bishops stood by their leader, and Thomas refused the King's proposal.

For the next three days the Bishops sat in a separate room while the King talked with his barons in the great hall, gradually working himself into one of his appalling rages. At intervals various eminent men dropped in on the Bishops to repeat his threats, while the head of the Templars in England and the French Abbot of l'Aumone reminded them that these alleged customs might not be so terrible after all; Henry was a Christian King, and a faithful supporter of the rightful Pope. But Henry only remembered that Thomas had promised to give way at the next public council, and his rage was fearful to behold. The Bishops of Salisbury and Norwich were already under his displeasure for other reasons; they genuinely feared that he might hang or blind them, and begged Thomas to yield. Yet all the Bishops stood together very gallantly; they might urge their leader to surrender, but they would not retreat until he gave the word.

On the third day Thomas suddenly yielded. He asked no advice, and the Bishops did not even know what he was about to do until he had done it. He strode into the great hall, swore to observe the ancient customs of the realm, and ordered the Bishops to follow his example.

But that evening he said bitterly that against his better judgement, and in obedience to the Pope's command, he had sworn more than a conscientious Archbishop could observe, and that very soon he would be doing penance for perjury.

After he had obtained this all-embracing oath of obedience Henry produced a document containing what he considered should be for the future the ancient customs of the realm, the famous Constitutions of Clarendon. Besides his new procedure for the hanging of convicted clerks he went back to the practice of William the Conqueror in the matter of appeals to Rome, disregarding the customs of King Stephen which had been in force for the last thirty years. The English Church was to be cut off from Christendom as a whole, and not even Papal letters addressed to every Christian might be published in England without the King's permission.

When Thomas saw this appalling document he refused to affix his seal to it, in spite of his oath. After plenty of plain speaking on both sides he left the King's presence, now convinced that he had committed the sin of perjury. Henry's mother, the Empress Matilda, was still living quietly in France. Someone asked her what she thought of the Constitutions, and she at once put her finger on the vital spot. It was one thing, she said, for the King to tell his Archbishop not to permit a particular case to go to Rome; all Kings did that, and it was a good custom; but to put the custom into *writing*, and force the Archbishop to swear to a code which conflicted with Canon Law, was tyranny; custom should never be written, for it changes continually with the times.

Thomas rode home in great distress, very near a ner-

vous breakdown. What worried him most was that everyone assumed he had yielded from fear; he was sensitive
to reflections on his courage, as was natural in a Norman
warrior. Actually he had hoped to keep the peace, in
accordance with the Pope's wishes; but he was not by
nature a peace-maker and he had landed himself in a hope-
less muddle. He had surrendered everything in dispute,
but so unwillingly and ungraciously that the King was
more hostile than ever.

For the next few months worry clouded his judgement,
and he did everything wrong. He first decided he had
committed the grave sin of perjury, and suspended himself from saying Mass until he had been absolved by his
only superior, the Pope. (When a later Archbishop of
Canterbury, Abbot, suspended himself for the grave sin
of homicide, having accidentally killed a beater out
shooting, there was no superior to absolve him until
King James I undertook the responsibility as Supreme
Head and Governor of the Church of England.) Alexander was unsympathetic, and wrote telling him not to be
silly. He then resolved that he must see the Pope, though
he had just sworn not to leave England without the King's
permission. He tried to flee secretly from his own town
of Romney, but bad weather forced him back. Word
came to the King that the Archbishop was seeking voluntary exile; he was delighted to hear it, and at once sent
knights to take possession of all the property of Canterbury. When they reached the episcopal palace they found
the Archbishop sitting morose in a corner of his hall, wet
through from his unsuccessful voyage. They returned, for
they had no power to disturb him while he remained lawfully in England. But his enemies mocked this ridiculous

clerk, who promised not to run away and could not even cross the Channel when he broke his promise.

The Bishops had lost confidence in the leader who had given in without consulting them, and were prepared to work the Constitutions. Thomas would not recognize the Constitutions, but neither would he take action against them; it seemed he would do nothing but sit at home and sulk. The new rules forbade an appeal to Rome, and no one proposed to break them. The King had won everything he wanted. But he was not content with victory; he desired the approval of Christendom in general, which at present regarded him as a tyrant. Of his own accord he did what no one else was permitted to do, and laid the Constitutions of Clarendon before the Pope.

That reopened the whole question. Since an appeal had been laid the Archbishop might lawfully take part in it. Pope Alexander himself formally sought his opinion, though since he considered himself in mortal sin for accepting these Constitutions his opinion might easily be guessed. The Pope, when at last he read the document, was profoundly shocked. He was prepared to concede the hanging of felonious clerks; ideally it was wrong but in a fallen world temporal rulers would hang murderers and escheat their property in spite of the Canons. Hitherto he had suspected that a lawyer-Archbishop was making a fuss over trivialities; but he saw that if appeals to the Curia were forbidden there would be no discipline in the English Church. He formally condemned the Constitutions, and forbade any clerk to observe them.

The King knew that Thomas was his only important antagonist. If he could be crushed the other Bishops would subside. But he also knew that Thomas would never again yield to threats, and that if he provoked a head-on collision over a matter of principle he might be driven into hanging his Archbishop, to the scandal of Christendom. He decided to catch Thomas in some breach of the secular law, where no principle was at stake.

The Archbishop of Canterbury was, among other things, a great baron, and like other great barons he presided over a court to which his free vassals brought their disputes. An appeal lay to the King's court if he denied justice to his tenants. One John the Marshal, an unimportant cadet of a noble family, claimed lands in the manor of Pagenham, part of the Honour of Canterbury. He lost his claim before the Archbishop, and appealed to the King's court. But in the course of bringing his appeal he had to swear, with the Gospels in his hand, that he had been denied justice; and of course the courts of the middle ages only functioned at all, even though they functioned badly, because even wicked men feared to risk Hell-fire by committing perjury on the Gospels. Instead of swearing on the book which the court offered him John produced what he said was his own copy; but afterwards it was discovered that he had sworn on a 'troper', a kind of hymn-book. John said he couldn't read and didn't know the difference; but any lawyer could see he was trying to deceive the court while avoiding the sin of swearing falsely on the Gospels. However, the King decided there was a case for the Archbishop to answer, and Thomas was summoned to appear on the 15th of September.

He might have sent a lawyer to represent him, or he might have asked for a postponement because he was too ill to attend; that was the usual answer to any summons, the chief reason why medieval trials lasted for years. As a matter of fact he was genuinely ill, probably from worry. But he disregarded the summons entirely, and when the day came and no one appeared in his name judgement was of course given against him. He had broken the law, and the law would no longer protect him. He was at the King's mercy, and now he must obey the King's summons to hear what 'amercement' was inflicted, or the King might send soldiers to fetch him by force.

He was summoned to appear before the King at the castle of Northampton on Tuesday the 6th of October 1164.

CHAPTER EIGHT

NORTHAMPTON

Northampton Castle was a comfortable modern building, a stone keep containing rooms on two floors with a staircase in a corner turret, as in the Tower of London at the present day; there was apparently only one gate to the outer enclosure or 'bailey', which surrounded the kitchen and stables and the flimsy wooden sheds where the lower orders slept. It was not quite so convenient for a conference as the rambling hunting-lodge of Clarendon, but at least there were separate committee-rooms where the parties might consult in private; some old-fashioned castles had only one living-room, which made privacy impossible.

The town was on the regular circuit of the hard-riding royal court, and already familiar to Thomas; he had recently met Henry outside the walls, in an effort to patch up their friendship; they rode apart for a private conversation, but the fierce war-horses on which both were mounted began to fight, and they had to change horses to continue the fruitless conversation. This serves to remind us that in the middle ages great men were nearly always mounted whenever they were out of doors, and that Thomas, even when Archbishop, habitually rode a fierce war-horse. In a town regularly visited by the court each great man would have his accustomed lodging (when the King of Scotland visited his suzerain fitting him in meant that everyone must move down one, amid violent recriminations); and Thomas went straight to the monastery of St. Andrew. He arrived in good time, for though he had put himself in the wrong over John the Marshal, and must receive sentence, he was determined to speak out before he was condemned.

But the King hawked by every stream on his journey, and reached Northampton two days late; perhaps he hoped Thomas would weaken under the strain of waiting, or perhaps he was genuinely trying to cool down, so that he would manage to keep his temper when the meeting opened.

On Thursday the 8th the court assembled, and Thomas rode to the castle with his crossbearer and his train of clerks, in the full state of an Archbishop. The distance was only a few hundred yards, but it would have looked very odd if he had arrived on foot. Apparently there was first a formal meeting in the great hall on the ground floor, and then Thomas and his clerks retired to a little room off the hall while the great men of the kingdom went upstairs to consider their judgement.

There was no doubt that Thomas was guilty of contempt of court in neglecting to attend on the 15th of September. In feudal eyes that was a very serious offence, for to refuse a summons to your lord's court was normally the first act of defiance which ended with open rebellion. But though everyone admitted in informal conversation that something ought to be done about it there was great reluctance to pass sentence on an Archbishop. The Bishops and Abbots, who sat as barons by virtue of their landed endowments, were the first to spy a loophole of escape.

They said that they had all sworn obedience to Canterbury, and it was a principle of feudal law that a vassal might never pass judgement on his lord. They left the court, and while some of them stood about chatting in the great hall many joined Thomas and his clerks in the 'solar', the name for a little room where you might be *solus* or alone. A party was beginning to form in his favour.

Left to themselves, the laymen made up their minds to finish off thoroughly a distasteful piece of business. The suitors of a feudal court were much more than a jury; not only did they find the verdict, they also announced the penalty, and if the sentence provoked resistance they were morally obliged to help in carrying it out by force. Now the barons decided that Thomas was at the King's mercy, and that the appropriate penalty was the forfeiture of all his chattels, his moveable property, everything except the land with which his See was endowed. The King was satisfied with this very severe sentence, and all that remained was to notify Thomas of the decision.

There were no volunteers for an errand which might very well incur immediate excommunication; but at last Henry of Winchester, King Stephen's brother and the senior Bishop in England, agreed to undertake it. Since he had refused to make one of the court no one could hold him responsible for the sentence. He informed Thomas that he had lost all his money and moveable property, and then at once went back to the King and offered all the wealth of Winchester as a guarantee that the Archbishop would pay honestly after he had returned to Canterbury and arranged his affairs; all the Bishops joined in this guarantee, except Gilbert Foliot of London, who now came out in his true colours as a disappointed rival and deadly enemy. That was the end of the case of John the Marshal; probably most barons hoped it would be the end of the case against the Archbishop, who must now return to Canterbury and live very quietly on the hospitality of the monks, without a horse or a silver spoon to his name. John and his two sons died within the year, which proved, at least to his contemporaries, that he had been guilty of perjury. The barons were not very happy to see a great man so heavily punished on appeal from his feudal court to the King's court, for they had feudal courts of their own. But before the meeting broke up the King announced that Thomas must attend on the next day to account for the money which had passed through his hands when he was Chancellor.

That proved that Henry was seeking vengeance, not justice. He knew Thomas had been careless in mixing government money with his private income, but he also knew the money had been spent on the War of Toulouse; even the profuse splendour of the embassy to Paris and the extravagance of the Chancellor's daily life had been in accordance with his own wishes, since the magnificence of the servant reflected glory on his master. Spitefulness apart, he knew he was asking the impossible; Thomas had been summoned to answer John the Marshal, and could not be expected to produce records of how he had paid 700 knights five years ago, without even a day's warning. If the accounts had in fact been written down, which is doubtful, they would be among the archives of the chancery; but Thomas was not granted time even to search his private papers at Canterbury; he must answer on Friday the 9th of October.

During the night Henry must have looked through some file concerned with the finances of the Archbishopric. For when the court opened next morning he began by announcing that Thomas would no longer administer the Honours of Eye and Berkhamstead; these had been granted during the King's pleasure while he was Chancellor, and then presumably forgotten. (An Honour was a complex of manors which had once belonged to the same baron; after it had come into the King's hands, forfeited for rebellion or escheated for lack of heirs, it was still administered as a separate unit.) That of course was not a punishment, merely the withdrawal of a royal favour; but it shows the inefficiency of medieval bookkeeping. The quarrel had begun at Westminster exactly a year ago, and during that year Henry had not noticed, nor had his clerks informed him, that Thomas was drawing at the King's pleasure the income of two great Honours. It makes the demand for five-year-old accounts all the more unreasonable.

But Thomas was legally accountable. The only answer he could make was to plead for time to examine the records at Canterbury. The King refused an adjournment of any length, but he permitted the Archbishop to withdraw and consult his friends, on condition his answer was ready next morning. It was customary for a defendant to give bail for his reappearance before he was permitted to leave the court, but the King remembered that Thomas had already forfeited all his chattels and was legally penniless; the Bishop of Winchester saved the situation by offering a bond for 2,000 marks. (3 marks = £2.)

This fairly simple quarrel seems to have taken up most of the short October day. The King had made a rhetorical speech of accusation, Thomas replied at considerable length, and the Bishop of Winchester dwelt on the blessings of concord and brotherly love. Presumably other members of the council expressed their views fully, for the whole dispute moved to an accompaniment of futile peace-making; Thomas and Henry were angry and obstinate, but the supporters of both sides were continually trying to find a face-saving formula. It was evening when Thomas returned to St. Andrews.

Early on Saturday morning the Bishops and Abbots of England called at the monastery to draw up some conciliatory answer which might appease the King. Every experienced politician realized that Henry and Thomas were both such violent and effective speakers that every time they met face to face they deepened the bitterness of the quarrel; the only chance of peace was to keep the protagonists apart while embassies rode between monastery and castle. The Bishop of Winchester was by far the wealthiest man in England, ruler of the richest See and brother to a King; his fixed idea was that Henry would do anything for money, if only they offered him enough; he was trying to work out how much he could raise when Thomas pointed out that Canterbury had already forfeited all its chattels, the Bishops had guaranteed payment from their own resources, and Winchester had put up a bond for 2,000 marks; if they went on at this rate not Canterbury only, but the whole English Church, would lose its endowments. The idea of buying the King's goodwill was abandoned.

Then the Bishop of Winchester recalled the solemn quittance which the Young King had granted at Thomas's election; he had proposed it himself, and though it probably meant nothing, as I have already pointed out, it offered the King an opportunity to give way gracefully, if he would be content with the chattels of Canterbury. That was all he would get anyway, since it was all Thomas possessed; if he demanded more it was only as an excuse to imprison his Archbishop. The Bishops and Abbots jumped at this straw, and rode off in a body to bring it to the King's attention. Thomas also entrusted them with another plea for an adjournment, if their first effort should fail.

The King would not recognize the quittance; his reasons were not reported and apparently he did nothing but bluster at large; though he was probably within his rights. But the Bishop of London shocked his colleagues by taking sides against his Archbishop, and that may have helped Henry to his decision. Foliot had a reputation as a wit, and apparently he could not bottle up an epigram which flashed through his mind. 'Our worthy Metropolitan', he said, 'seems to think consecration as Bishop washes away debt, as baptism washes away sin.' This was not exactly Thomas's position, but it was true enough to be funny and wounding.

The King was persuaded to grant an adjournment over the week-end, but he refused permission for Thomas to visit his office in Canterbury. He must remain in Northampton, and present his accounts on Monday.

The Bishops returned to St. Andrews, and the evening was spent in discussing plans for the future. Everyone saw that the King was determined to crush Thomas; he had the physical force to do it, and it would be done; but if the Archbishop of Canterbury were hanged or shut up in a dungeon that would be the signal for unrelenting war between Church and State; was there any way to preserve the peace? The Bishop of Winchester, a sound churchman but elderly and rather too anxious for peace at any price, suggested that Thomas should resign his Archbishopric and go into exile as a private individual. Then some other Archbishop might be elected, and the King would cease to harass the Church. The idea was attractive. Obviously the source of the King's rancour was his personal hatred of the clerk who had once been his friend and now opposed his plan for the subjection of the Church to the laity; the Pope had shown himself willing to tolerate about half the Constitutions of Clarendon, and skilful diplomatists might invent some formula to cover the other half if both sides genuinely sought peace. While the Emperor held Rome for his Antipope it was important to keep the King of England as a supporter of Alexander III. Many Bishops and Abbots thought resignation would save the situation; Thomas himself did not dismiss the proposal out of hand, but sat down to think it over.

He knew that the best he could hope for was exile; he would never again lead 700 knights or go hawking in state, whatever happened. But with the prestige of a persecuted Confessor who had resigned a great position in the cause of peace he might expect a pleasant life in Paris or Bologna, or as the honoured guest of some wealthy monastery. It was not regard for his own dignity which made him refuse. His keen legal mind examined the proposal and saw that it would set a precedent fatal to the freedom of the English Church. Most Archbishops quarrelled with the King at one time or another; it might be called an occupational risk of their calling. If it was established that an Archbishop should resign when requested Canterbury would be held at the King's pleasure, like the Honour of Berkhamstead; Henry would change Archbishops until he found a really subservient retainer who would be kept in order by the threat of dismissal. The Church would be leaderless under the lay sword, and he would have none of it. Henry of Winchester and the other Bishops agreed with his reasons when he had explained them.

The court did not meet on Sunday the 11th of October. At St. Andrews the day passed in futile haverings with Bishops and Abbots. We must not draw too firm a line between Church and State; most of these eminent clerks were related to lay magnates, as was the Abbot of Battle; they knew they must stand up for the rights of the Church, and of course they were just as brave personally as the warriors their cousins; but they dreaded to be forced into a position where they would have to excommunicate most of the King's followers or be excommunicated themselves; surely, even at this late hour, there must be some way of making peace between King and Church?

Thomas found these endless circular arguments very trying; his only friend among the laity had been King Henry himself, and if he could cut himself off from the loved companion of his youth because his duty demanded it, surely his subordinates should not baulk at unpleasant family differences? He was also in grave personal danger, as his clerks frequently reminded him. Once the King had been barely restrained from tearing out with his own hands the eyes of a groom who delivered an impudent message; if the argument grew hot he was capable of drawing his sword and cutting down his adversary.

Then, was he justified in continuing a quarrel which must lead to excommunication, probably interdict, a complete cessation of the Christian life of England? As Archbishop his first duty was to save souls, not to inhibit every altar in the country for the sake of appeals to Rome, appeals which had been frequently forbidden in the past. The right of appeal had never been unquestioned, and anyway, the tempter whispered, after Henry was dead another Pope would win it back from the next King who sought clerical support against powerful rebels. Thomas was proud, headstrong, and quick-tempered; but he was conscious of his faults, as his hair-shirt bears witness; perhaps he was being led by his fiery Norman pride into factious opposition, when a really holy man would have thought first of peace? On that Sunday evening he began to wonder, for the first time, whether he was completely in the right. He worried until he made himself really ill, and on Monday morning was confined to his bed with 'the iliac passion', a piece of contemporary medical jargon which may mean anything from a heart-attack to stomach-ache. In this case it was probably nervous indigestion.

The King of course took it for granted he was playing for time, like any other defendant who must lose his case. But the Bishops reported it as a genuine case of illness, and Thomas sent a message saying one day in bed would put him right, and promising that he would be at the castle, without fail, on Tuesday morning. The court therefore adjourned to Tuesday.

For Thomas had now made up his mind, and the decision brought peace. Disregarding all considerations of prudence and personal safety, he had consulted his confessor about the bare rights and wrongs of the matter.

Prior Robert of Merton was as tough as his old school-fellow, and this was his advice: 'If you desire success in this world, make peace with the King. But if you wish to serve God, act fearlessly. St. Stephen, who spoke fear-lessly before the council of the Jews, is patron of those who speak fearlessly before Kings; let your Mass to-morrow be a votive Mass in his honour.'

Thomas could always be persuaded by an appeal to his courage; at once his mind was at rest and his body began to heal. But he knew that to-morrow would be his last chance of making clear his position before the people of England, for by nightfall he could be either a prisoner or a fugitive; he prepared for the climax of his trial with all the flamboyant stage-management he had shown at his state entry into Paris.

On the 13th he rose early to say his votive Mass, which opens with the 118th Psalm as Introit, 'Princes also did sit and speak against me; but Thy servant is occupied in Thy statutes.' During Mass many of the Bishops arrived, and were surprised to see the red vestments he wore in honour of the first martyr; for the 13th of October is the feast of St. Edward the Confessor, when white is usually worn. They thought the colour a very bad omen.

After Mass Thomas addressed the assembled Bishops, and ordered them, by the obedience they had sworn to Canterbury, to excommunicate anyone who laid hands on the consecrated person of an Archbishop. He also gave public notice that he appealed to Rome (in breach of the Constitutions) against any sentence which the King's court might impose. As I have already explained, this system of appealing before sentence was quite normal at that time; Gilbert of London followed his example by giving notice of appeal against the Archbishop's order to excommunicate those who might carry out the lawful commands of the King; which meant that he need not obey the order until the Pope decided.

The Bishops then rode to the castle, where they must take their places as suitors of the court; though they would excuse themselves on the usual feudal plea when their lord the Archbishop appeared before it. But Salisbury and Winchester, who were personal friends as well as colleagues, remained to encourage him.

Thomas proposed to ride to his trial wearing full Mass-vestments under the cope and pallium of an Archbishop. That was altogether too theatrical, and his friends persuaded him to exercise restraint. He compromised by wearing cope and pallium over his usual black Augustinian gown, though he insisted on hanging his stole round his neck and carrying the Blessed Sacrament in a pyx, that he might administer Communion to himself if he was condemned to immediate execution. We know that he got away safely, and even some contemporary eye-witnesses thought he was making an hysterical fuss; but he was actually in danger of death, though on that occasion he escaped it, and he was entitled to dramatize his plight to influence public opinion.

He rode to the castle in the full state of an Archbishop, with his train of clerks around him and his cross borne before. This cross, a tall metal pole topped with a crucifix, was the symbol of his authority over all the diocesan Bishops, clerks and laity of the Province of Canterbury; it would remind the barons what manner of man they were judging.

He rode into the bailey of the castle through the fortified gate, which was immediately locked behind him, a very unpleasant portent. When he reached the stairway leading to the door of the keep he dismounted, and then walked over and took the cross from the hands of the astonished cross-bearer. There was a flurry of excitement among the onlookers. The Bishops of London and Hereford were standing by the door, and a clerk said to Foliot, 'My lord of London, can you stand by while the Archbishop carries his cross with his own hands?' To which Gilbert answered, 'My dear fellow, that man always was a fool, and he always will be.' He had a genuine intellectual contempt for these theatrical displays, but he was also trying to put Thomas in the wrong to serve his new master, King Henry.

As Thomas entered the door the saintly Robert of Melun, Bishop of Hereford, stepped forward to relieve him of his cross, from respect for his Metropolitan; at the same time Gilbert tried to snatch it, saying angrily: 'If you brandish your cross the King will brandish his sword. Then who shall make peace between you?'

'The cross is the emblem of peace,' Thomas replied. 'I carry it for the protection of the whole English Church.'

Probably he carried it rather as though it were the lance with which he had unhorsed Engelram de Trie; in any case he grasped it firmly; neither Bishop could wrest it from him, and he swept on, still bearing it, right through the great hall of the castle and into the little solar beyond it, on the ground floor. There he sat quietly, the cross between his knees; only two of his clerks had the courage to sit with him in the stronghold of his bitter and powerful foe.

The court was not yet assembled; the King was sitting

with a few companions in the corresponding solar on the
floor above, and there was a pause in the proceedings.
The next important man to arrive was Roger Archbishop
of York; we are told he came late on purpose, for two
reasons: he was known to be hostile to Thomas, and
hoped sentence would be pronounced before he arrived,
so that he might avoid the awkwardness of passing
judgement on a personal enemy; and he was very vain,
and always arrived late at important meetings so as to be
sure of a crowd of spectators for his procession. He had
never sworn obedience to Canterbury, and therefore
might remain a member of the court. But his vanity led
him to have his cross borne before him, which was only
allowed in his own Province of York, and the southern
Bishops were angered at the sight. It seemed very striking
that there should be two Metropolitan crosses under one
roof, and a clerk whispered to Thomas that they seemed
like two lances in rest before a bloody joust.

The Bishops went upstairs for a last appeal to the King
before the court assembled. We must remember that even
those Bishops hostile to Thomas, like York and London,
did not wish to see him condemned. They wanted the
King to win, but on points, not by a knock-out; and if
Thomas would only yield peacefully that would be the
best solution of all.

But the King had a new grievance; it had just come to
his ears that, in spite of the Constitutions of Clarendon,
his Bishops had spent the morning appealing to Rome
against one another. Presumably Gilbert of London apolo-
gized and was forgiven, and then the King sent some of
his courtiers downstairs to order Thomas to withdraw his
appeal. A group of gay young warriors delivered the

message, and then stood chatting in the doorway; but
their chatter was very pointed; they recalled how William
the Conqueror had imprisoned the Bishop of Bayeux in a
very severe dungeon, and how Count Geoffrey of Anjou,
father to the present King, had taken an appalling vengeance on a whole group of clerks because one of them
had dared to be elected Bishop of Seez without his consent. These young courtiers were church-going Christians,
like everyone else in twelfth-century England; they could
not in cold blood cut down an Archbishop, but they were
working themselves into the frame of mind in which they
could.

Thomas refused to withdraw his appeal, or to take any
notice of the threatening conversation. Since making
threats to a man who pays no attention is a dull amusement, and can even be embarrassing, the courtiers presently went back upstairs to the King. It is worth noting
that all through this day, the crucial day of the Council of
Northampton, Thomas and Henry never met face to face;
responsible statesmen took great pains to keep them apart,
for they knew that if two such fiery-tempered warriors
began to bandy insults at a range of a few feet the alterca-
tion would probably end in murder.

As the day wore on nervous deputations continually
scampered up and down the stairs, reporting the King's
rage to Thomas, and the Archbishop's immovable obstinacy to Henry. Presently Roger of York left the King's
solar and began to mobilize his ceremonial train of clerks,
who were discussing the crisis with other hangers-on in
the great hall; he put his head in the door of the lower
solar and made a final appeal for peace; Thomas only
answered, 'Get thee behind me, Satan'. Roger then ad-

dressed his clerks in a loud voice, explaining that he was leading them out of the castle at once because no clerk should witness the terrible things that would be done to the Archbishop of Canterbury in the next few minutes.

This may have been yet another attempt to frighten Thomas; but Roger had known him intimately since they were both rising young men in Theobald's family, and he must have realized that Thomas could not be frightened. More probably he did expect murder or blinding very soon; he departed at the most exciting stage of the proceedings because it was pointed out to him that if he was present when harm came to his bitterest enemy and rival, rumour would accuse him of being the ringleader. His position was that of all the clerks of the King's party: he wanted Thomas Becket to be suppressed in some undefined way, and yet the solidarity of the clergy to their order made him hope that no layman would lay hands on the Archbishop of Canterbury.

Thomas had now reached a heroic stage of anger, and was quite ready for martyrdom. The only chance for the peace-makers was to work on his affection for others, reminding him that he would not be the only sufferer in a conflict between Church and State. Henry of Winchester had consecrated him, which gave him some of the status of a lord and patron; he begged him to resign and go abroad, to save his old comrade in arms and loved companion from the sin of sacrilege and murder. Bartholomew Bishop of Exeter, a distinguished Doctor of Paris, fell on his knees in an agony of fear and begged him not to bring down the royal vengeance on them all; but he was the only Bishop whose nerve failed him on that terrible day. Thomas sat like a statue, clasping his cross;

his only answer was that he had appealed to the Pope, and that if judgement went against him he would give way at once. Henry of Winchester once more climbed the stairs and cunningly reminded Gilbert of London and Hilary of Chichester, who were advising the King, that if Thomas was killed while they were in the same castle they would never clear themselves from suspicion of murder; Roger of York had seen that point already; they were more concerned than anyone that the council should have a bloodless ending.

Gilbert and Hilary were trained lawyers, skilful politicians, and experienced men of the world. They watched the King closely, and made their proposal when he was too excited and angry to think out its implications; they suggested that they should appeal to the Pope in the name of all the Bishops of England, saying Thomas had proved himself unfit for his office and begging Alexander to depose him. Henry accepted, seeing only the resounding insult to Thomas which such an appeal would be. He did not notice that he was once again conceding the right of appeal to the Pope, who had nullified the Constitutions of Clarendon just when the English Church had been bullied into accepting them.

That disposed of the first item on the agenda. Thomas could no longer be required to withdraw his appeal, since his suffragans were appealing against him. The King's court could proceed to trial.

The Bishops took their places in court, to ensure recognition of their right to be present. But as usual they immediately withdrew. Those who had supported their Archbishop joined Thomas in his solar; for the first time that day he relaxed and chatted with his equals. He was now much calmer, for nothing further was required of him; the case had gone on appeal to the court whose protection he had always sought, and until the Pope gave judgement he might stand idle.

Evidently the keep of Northampton was built with two identical storeys, for the King's court met on the first floor, not in the great hall which Thomas could see through the open door of his solar. He and his companions heard the angry roar of that mass-meeting of excited warriors, but they could not distinguish the formal words of accusation and sentence. In fact we do not know the charge on which he was accused. But the King's vassals were enraged at the long-drawn defiance of the Archbishop, and they all shouted 'Traitor' as soon as they were asked for an opinion. Sentence was passed by acclamation, but again we do not know what it was; probably imprisonment for life. The next formal step in the proceedings was for the court to inform the culprit of his sentence; the barons trooped downstairs to the great hall, shouting threats and abuse.

But at the open door of the solar they checked, seeing the Archbishop in cope and pallium, his cross in his hands, surrounded by his faithful suffragans and clerks. They were the grandsons of the heroes who stormed Antioch and Jerusalem, and their sons would follow Richard Lionheart to Acre; they took it for granted that once in his life every gentleman would journey to Outremer to fight for God's Church; they were the King's servants, but God's also, as was every knight in that spring-time of chivalry. They dared not pass sentence on a consecrated Bishop.

After a good deal of pushing and jostling the Earl of

Leicester unwillingly came forward and began to speak. He rambled on at length about the temporal sword of justice, and the duty of clerks to obey their secular rulers, whose office also was of divine origin, with other commonplaces of the Ghibelline position; but presently he began to stammer from sheer embarrassment, and subsided into silence before he had pronounced the sentence of the court.

The Earl of Cornwall tried next, but he also broke down before reaching the point.

This ridiculous hold-up in the proceedings was very trying to the tempers of those chiefly concerned. Thomas had kept his self-possession when he heard the cries of 'Traitor' from the floor above, but as layman after layman harangued him on his duty as Archbishop he began to grow very angry. However, Hilary of Chichester was the first to lose his temper and his head; he had hated Thomas ever since he lost his suit against Battle Abbey, and at last everything was going exactly as he had wished; Thomas would be imprisoned in a dungeon where he could not exercise his Metropolitan powers, and presently the Pope would certainly depose an Archbishop who had quarrelled with every authority in his Province; the sentence must be delivered without delay. He thrust himself forward, and said in formal Latin that the Archbishop was manifestly a traitor and must hear what the court had decided.

Thomas, the trained lawyer, at once seized on this flaw. If he could avoid sentence and actual imprisonment he might rouse the public opinion of Christendom against this persecution of the English Church. He rose, shouting that no Bishop might pronounce sentence on his own

Metropolitan, and strode to the door, carrying his cross. The crowd fell back before his wrath.

This was a very critical moment. He had not been sentenced, and therefore he was still technically at liberty. But he was fleeing the court which had judged him, and any suitor was entitled to arrest him. If the King had been present, or if anyone else had come forward to assume command, he would certainly have been seized; but no one wished to incur the severest form of excommunication by laying hands, without direct orders, on a consecrated Bishop; even his bitterest enemies only wanted to be rid of him, and were not sorry to see him go. All day they had been pleading with him to resign, and if he fled that would come to the same thing. But it was touch and go. As he strode down the long hall those before him shrank from his flashing eyes and menacing gestures; but those who saw only his back picked up rushes from the floor to pelt him, shouting rude epithets. The Earl of Warenne was particularly offensive; but he was the King's bastard half-brother, and bastards should never begin an exchange of insults, since it is so easy to answer them in kind. There are various versions of Thomas's reply, though he certainly proclaimed that but for his priesthood he would have killed the young man in a duel. The Earl was silenced, and oddly enough he conceived a great admiration for the Archbishop's courage and holiness; years later he invoked the holy martyr St. Thomas of Canterbury, and was immediately cured of some trouble in his eyes.

Thomas swept through the hall, keeping the knights at bay by the pride of his demeanour, as a lion-tamer dominates his beasts; as he neared the door, his head high, he stumbled over a heap of firewood; that was the most dangerous moment, for some onlookers laughed; if the crowd as a whole had thought him ridiculous he would have been lost. But he gained the door safely, with his two clerks, and hurried down the steps to the courtyard.

A row of horses stood tethered by the outer gate, but the gate itself was locked and the porter absent. There was not a moment to lose. Thomas went straight to his horse and mounted, for such a keen hawker and warrior probably recognized individual horses more easily than human beings; but Herbert of Bosham, his chaplain, dithered up and down the line of strange rumps until Thomas ordered him to jump up behind; his war-horse could easily carry two unmailed riders. The other clerk shook the locked gate, and then snatched at a bunch of keys he saw hanging nearby; the first key he thrust into the lock opened the gate, which was certainly very lucky and was generally accounted a miracle; he found his horse quickly, and before the King, still in his solar upstairs, could give orders for arrest the two horses were galloping with their three riders through the streets of Northampton.

Once in the monastery of St. Andrews they were safe. The King would hesitate to violate the sanctuary, and the burgesses could be relied on to give timely warning if soldiers set out to arrest him; burgesses usually supported the Church against the King. Thomas relaxed, and went to supper in the refectory. (Apparently on this eventful day he missed his dinner.)

The King very sensibly proclaimed that the Archbishop was under his personal protection, and must on no account be molested; he relied on the strong case he could put before the Pope, and did not wish to weaken it by unauthorized reprisals. As soon as this was known both parties among the Bishops renewed their efforts to patch up a peace. London and Chichester, adversaries to Thomas, called to suggest that if he offered the King the lands of Canterbury as well as its chattels he might live undisturbed as the guest of a monastery until the case had been decided. But Thomas, rightly, refused to disendow the See which it was his duty to hand on unimpaired to his eventual successor. When his friends, Worcester, Hereford and Rochester, called to express their sympathy he sent them to ask the King for a passport, since he wished to consult the Pope in his French exile; they came back about bedtime with the news that the King would not give a definite answer; he wished to sleep on the matter and pronounce his decision later.

There was then a discussion about the morality or flight in time of persecution, for some theologians held that a Bishop should stand by his flock to the last. Someone adduced a telling argument from Holy Writ. St. Peter stayed by Our Lord even after His arrest, and went of his own accord to the house of the High Priest; but his courage could not stand the strain and he was driven to denying his master. St. John, though he was the Beloved Disciple, escaped while he could and never committed the sin of denial. Therefore, since no man can know in advance that he will have the courage to endure martyrdom, it is permissible for even a Bishop to flee. Thomas made up his mind to escape.

But he did not wish to implicate the monks of St. Andrews. He explained that he was worn out by the events of the day, much too tired to rise for Matins at midnight; but the sound of the holy psalms would comfort him; could he have a bed made up within the chapel, where he might hear the office while he rested? A bed was placed behind the High Altar, near the choir but actually hidden from the monks. At midnight Thomas rose, slipped out of the chapel, and joined the faithful Herbert of Bosham who held two horses in the street outside. (If the monks kept their rule strictly, and St. Andrews had that reputation, he must have climbed the enclosure wall, since all outer doors would be locked for the night.) The King had ordered the burgesses of Northampton to guard their gates, for fear of disturbances in the unsettled state of public feeling. But by a remarkable coincidence, which some thought a miracle, there had been a muddle about posting the sentries; the north gate, which Thomas tried first, was the only one open and unguarded. I think myself that the guard-commander had heard a rumour, and was glad to see the cause of what might be a bloody quarrel ride away from his peaceful town.

With only one companion Thomas rode openly, but swiftly, to the town of Lincoln, and on to the neighbouring Gilbertine monastery of Haverholm. There he 'went underground', though the King was not in fact looking for him very hard. He left Haverholm wearing the cowl of a Gilbertine canon, the only native English order, and riding the kind of nag appropriate to a travelling cleric instead of his own excellent war-horse. In this disguise he made his way slowly through East Anglia and Essex to the small town of Eastry in Kent, which owed feudal obedience to Canterbury. There he got in touch with the fishermen of Sandwich (some contemporary records call them pirates, but they may have done a little fishing in their spare time), and eventually landed at St. Omer on the 4th of November, having disappeared from Northampton on the 14th of October.

CHAPTER NINE

SENS AND PONTIGNY

 King Henry ruled the coast of France from Normandy to the Pyrenees, and Thomas was compelled to land in Flanders. But he had opposed the marriage of the Count of Flanders with a professed nun, and he would not be safe until he reached the Ile de France, the district round Paris which had no other lord but King Louis. He decided to cross Flanders in disguise. It was the wisest course, but it entailed considerable hardship.

He was never alone in his wanderings. A few English clerks, we do not know how many, had accompanied him in the little fishing-boat; later legend described it as a dinghy, rowed by only two men, but that may be an exaggeration. To any clerk he could safely reveal his identity, and Flemish priests and monks guided the little party from one religious community to the next. But he was still disguised as a canon of the Gilbertine order and of course had no money to buy horses; and apparently it was the custom for Flemish monks to travel on foot, though in England they usually rode. Thomas was forced to walk long distances for the first time since he had entered the household of Archbishop Theobald twenty years ago; he was forty-six years of age, and he made very heavy weather of it.

Two anecdotes of this journey reveal something of his personality. After a long day of trudging over the shifting dunes, assisted by a horribly fishy walking-stick which a fisherman's wife had previously used to stir her stew-pans, he begged supper and shelter for the night at a little hut on the shore. The pious housewife gave the usual cauldron of boiled fish to the holy monks first of all, intending to eat what remained after they had finished; as she handed over the pot she noticed that the leader of the monks had the soft hands of a gentleman, and guessed he was some great lord escaping in disguise; but when he and his comrades had eaten a very little of the nasty food Thomas, without thinking, passed the pot to a beggar at the door; then she knew that he was not only a great lord but a great churchman, accustomed to giving the remains of his dinner to the poor at the gate; the only great churchman at present on the run was the missing Archbishop of Canterbury, and she knelt for his blessing. Thomas admitted his identity, and of course the poor fisherfolk kept his secret; though the Count of Flanders would have rewarded them richly if they had betrayed him.

But though the poor always sided with the Church against the State, gentlemen, even if they were devout Christians, were hampered by the duty they had sworn to their secular lords. The next time he was recognized Thomas was in greater danger. A knight rode along the shore, hawk on wrist, and as he passed a little group of travelling monks he noticed that their tall handsome leader looked the hawk over with the professional eye of a keen hunting man; that was odd, for hawking was a very technical business which could only be understood after long practice, and of course such a frivolous pastime was forbidden to monks. He noted how tall and dignified was this monkish hawk-fancier. Was there any tall, dignified sportsman who might be wandering through Flanders disguised as a monk? Of course, the Archbishop of Canterbury! But he feared to look foolish if he raised a false alarm, so he tested the soundness of his suspicion. As he rode by he called to the last member of the party, 'That brother in front knows too much about hawks for a holy monk. I suppose he isn't Archbishop Thomas in disguise?'

The quick-witted clerk, who was also a secular disguised as a monk, saved the situation. 'Have you ever seen Archbishop Thomas?' he answered. 'Well, at least you've heard the story of his famous embassy to Paris. Can you imagine such a lover of luxury trudging the dunes on foot? That is not how the Archbishop of Canterbury goes on a journey.'

The knight was convinced, and Thomas walked on safely.

At the present day many churches in Belgium treasure as holy relics magnificent chalices which are said to have been presented by the Archbishop in return for a night's lodging. But Thomas carried no baggage and was penniless. These may well be vessels he used at his morning Mass during the dangerous journey, but they must have been already the property of these Flemish churches, lent to a distinguished Archbishop for one morning; within ten years Thomas was canonized, and then they would be set apart as relics.

Passed on safely from monastery to monastery, Thomas eventually accomplished his harassing march. At Soissons he was under the protection of the King of France, and

Louis VII was a faithful servant of the Church. Thomas declared himself, and the King at once sent him horses, suitable robes, and a considerable escort; he might ride to the Pope at Sens in the accustomed state of an Archbishop.

As soon as he learned that Thomas had left the country King Henry had assumed he was on his way to the Pope. The obvious strategy was to open the appeal from the Bishops of England before he arrived. A representative delegation was sent to argue the case under the leadership of the Bishops of London and Chichester, eminent lawyers accustomed to speaking before the Curia, and bitter foes to Thomas; but it also included the Bishop of Worcester, who had supported his Archbishop at Northampton, and a number of secular magnates, to prove that every party in England was tired of the cantankerous and obstinate Primate. The Pope decided to hear the case in person, assisted of course by his Cardinals and Curia; and it was opened, as Henry had hoped, while Thomas was still at Soissons.

We are now about to embark on a tangle of legal proceedings which continued for six years and were never decided by a competent court. Two factors must be made clear at the outset: the issues at stake in each particular argument, and the extra-legal reasons of foreign and domestic policy which so largely influenced the opinions of both judges and parties. This particular appeal raised no issue of law, for the great principle that the Pope was the supreme judge in everything that affected the Church had been conceded when Henry sent his delegation. No one maintained that Thomas was not rightfully Archbishop, or that as Archbishop he had exceeded his powers;

the King's lawyers merely argued that he had shown himself unworthy of his great position, by quarrelling with the secular power and with most of his suffragans over what were really petty points of administration; and that it would be for the good of the Church in England if the Pope would translate him to some honorary Metropolitan See at present in the hands of the infidel, where he would have no subjects to misgovern. Let him end his days in a monastery as Archbishop of Something-opolis, while some other clerk who had the knack of handling the hot-tempered King ruled in Canterbury.

Henry might expect Alexander III to grant this request. The schismatic Emperor held Rome, and the Pope, who had very little money, was the guest of the King of France; but the French Church was traditionally very independent of Rome in the daily management of its affairs, especially its financial affairs; while the Church in England, which had been founded by Roman monks sent specially on that mission by Pope Gregory the Great, was accustomed to paying Peter's Pence and the first year's income of every newly-appointed Bishop, and many other imposts which were seldom paid on the Continent. Alexander was dependent on Henry for most of his ready cash, and it was reasonable to suppose that he would grant him a favour which raised no point of principle, a mere matter of administration.

In theory the King of France, lord of Sens and the generous host of the indigent Pope, should have been an important actor in the great controversy. He had very great prestige, and enough military power to fight on level terms against the Duke of Normandy and King of England. But the personal character of Louis VII lessened his importance. He was a gallant and chivalrous knight, who had raised a powerful contingent for the Second Crusade and then come home without in any way strengthening the imperilled baronies of Outremer because of his incompetence in diplomacy and his lack of energy as a warrior. His vassals admired his unswerving honesty, but regretted that his simplicity and good nature caused him to miss many obvious opportunities for the increase of his Kingly power. His attitude was simple and predictable. He was delighted to be host to the Pope, and would never incur the threat of excommunication by disobeying him in an important matter of faith or morals; but he was a King, and he had a fellow-feeling for Kings who quarrelled with obstreperous Archbishops. He wanted everyone to kiss and be friends as quickly as possible, and to attain this object he had great faith in the effects of a personal interview. He never understood that Henry and Thomas, who had once been so intimate, now got on each other's nerves and were better kept apart, though every English baron and Bishop had seen that at Northampton; he thought that if only he could get them riding side by side in the same field they would at once recover the friendly footing of five years ago.

Somewhere in the Rhineland was the Holy Roman Emperor, always tempting Henry to swear obedience to his schismatic Antipope. Then they could attack Louis from east and west simultaneously, and divide the Kingdom of France. Just to complicate matters, the Guelfs of the Lombard cities, who were maintaining a surprisingly successful rebellion against the Emperor's German army, were offering to make Henry King of Lombardy if he went to war on their side. Henry found both offers very tempting, but his vassals, already very heavily taxed, dreaded to see him drawn into the unending war between Guelf and Ghibelline, on either side. There were few official negotiations between England and the leaders in the great Lombard War, and therefore it escapes notice in most histories of England at this period; but the under-tow of secret bargaining continued, and sometimes affected Henry's position.

When the envoys of the English Bishops were ready to open their appeal Gilbert Foliot of London was chosen chief spokesman. He was the natural choice, for though Hilary of Chichester was an equally eminent lawyer Gilbert was also a monk of saintly private life, which it was hoped would influence Alexander. There was also the point that the Pope had often met Thomas, at the Council of Tours and in argument before the Curia when he was Archbishop Theobald's lawyer; it was said that the Pope liked and admired him. Alexander also knew Hilary of Chichester, for they had been colleagues in the Curia of a previous Pope; but it was notorious that he disliked him personally. The Bishop of London would start with a clean sheet.

But Gilbert took the wrong tone from the start. He began by saying that Thomas's election to Canterbury had been procured by royal pressure and was probably sim-oniacal; since the Pope had approved the appointment with enthusiasm this was lacking in tact. He went on to accuse Thomas of a scandalous private life, which every-one knew to be untrue, and added that he had thrown England into confusion by escaping secretly abroad when he was in no danger; he had not even waited to see whether the King would grant him permission to leave openly. That was a genuine point, for many Cardinals thought Thomas had been too hasty in abandoning his flock. But Gilbert was carried away by his own eloquence, and wound up a resounding period with the apt quotation from the Bible, 'the wicked flee when no man pursueth'.

Alexander interrupted with the words, 'Deal gently, my brother'. (All Bishops are brethren, and the Pope is Bishop of Rome.)

'Since you command it, I shall be gentle with him,' Gilbert answered politely, hastily recasting his next sentence.

'I do not ask you to deal gently with the Archbishop, but with your own argument, which is harmed by your violence,' was the devastating answer.

Gilbert soon stammered to a close. He had prepared a strong speech, and he could not while he was on his feet turn it into a gentle one. The English delegation turned automatically to Bishop Hilary; he was evidently the sort of man who can deliver a fluent speech on any subject at a moment's notice, though for this occasion he had relied on Gilbert and come into court with nothing prepared. He took up where his colleague had left off, dwelling on the particular wickedness of an Archbishop, of all people, being the disturber of concord. He noted that Thomas seldom consulted his lawful advisers, but announced important decisions suddenly, without talking them over beforehand; another sound point in the King's favour.

But I suppose on the journey from England Hilary had spent most of his time with the French-speaking barons, and it was many years since he had last made a speech before the Curia. He must have been thinking in French and translating as he went along, instead of thinking in the Latin he was speaking. He forgot that the Latin word *oportet* is an impersonal verb which must never be conjugated, and as he explained that the Archbishop's clerks ought never to have allowed him to behave as he did he invented a splendid new word, *oportuebant*. That was a ridiculous blunder, about equivalent to saying in English 'they used to ought'; some clerk of the Curia made it sound even funnier by calling out, 'That ship has found the wrong *port*'. (Perhaps there was a nautical flavour in the appearance of the Bishop of maritime Chichester.) The court dissolved in laughter, and the unfortunate and unpopular Hilary was too shaken to continue. We must remember that a Bishop continually prayed in Latin, wrote Latin, and read Latin; if he made mistakes in Latin grammar he would seem as ludicrous as a modern Bishop who could not read the Prayer Book.

The Earl of Leicester bravely stepped into the breach. But of course he couldn't speak Latin at all, and his French had to be translated for the benefit of the Italian Cardinals. He stammered a few brief and soldierly remarks, dwelling on the fact that all the King's loyal vassals considered Thomas a traitor, and had said so at Northampton. The Pope then adjourned the court, saying he must hear the Archbishop's defence before he announced his decision.

The King's party realized at once that the decision would go against them. In strict law they had no case against Thomas; they were envoys from a friendly King who was seeking a friendly favour, the translation of a tiresome Archbishop. As soon as Alexander talked of hearing the defence that showed he was thinking of the

Thomas Parting from Pope Alexander

From a French poem of about 1240, and therefore the costumes are not contemporary. But note that Pope and Archbishop ride like knights, their horses properly up to the bit; while the cross-bearer rides very pompously, and the Cardinals on the left sit like sacks. In the Middle Ages great men lived in the saddle, and most interviews took place on horseback

legal aspect. The English delegation left Sens before Thomas arrived, anxious to avoid an unpleasant encounter (for the clerks in the party had all at some time sworn obedience to the Archbishop).

When Thomas arrived Pope Alexander was very gracious, and made it clear that there was no intention of translating him. But the lawyers of the Curia had been much interested in one argument of Gilbert's; if the spokesman of a King said his master had used undue influence in the election of an Archbishop that was much too useful a weapon to be thrown away, even if it was unsound in this particular case. Thomas agreed that it was a valuable precedent, and he may also have felt a passing mood of weariness with the whole interminable quarrel; either because he wished to emphasize his loyalty and give the head of the Church a completely free hand, or to make it easier for Canterbury to be filled by free election in times to come, he pulled off the sacred ring which was his badge of office and tendered it to the Pope. Alexander solemnly replaced it on his finger. Thomas was now Archbishop of Canterbury by personal appointment from the Holy See, the strongest title in the world; no one in future might argue that his election was invalid, as procured by royal pressure.

The Papacy was continually negotiating with Kings, but the boundaries of secular Kingdoms did not always coincide with ecclesiastical Provinces; the Province of Lyons was half in France and half in the Holy Roman Empire, and not only was York independent of Canterbury but the Archbishop of York claimed to rule the Bishops of Scotland (though his claim was never conceded by the Scots, and formally abandoned in the next

generation). It was therefore the custom to choose some
Bishop to act as Papal Legate, with delegated authority
over the whole Church in one Kingdom, to enforce uni-
formity in the application of the particular compromise
between the conflicting claims of King and Pope which
had been agreed for that realm. In England the Legate
was normally the Archbishop of Canterbury, though this
had not yet become a hard-and-fast rule; Bishop Henry of
Winchester had been Legate to his brother King Stephen,
and about the time of the Council of Clarendon Roger of
York had been Legate in name, though with powers so
restricted that the office was in fact vacant; it was an
appointment granted at the Pope's pleasure, which he
might terminate without giving any reason.

The Pope, when he reinvested Thomas with his ring,
appointed him Legate in the Kingdom of England; that
gave him a claim to the obedience of York, and much
greater power over his suffragans than was enjoyed by an
ordinary Metropolitan; for example, he could excommunicate them or suspend them from exercising their
episcopal functions if they did not obey him as Legate,
while as Metropolitan his only remedy for disobedience
was to prosecute before the Roman Curia.

But Alexander regarded himself as the impartial judge
of a dispute between a Bishop and a King, not as the
pledged supporter of Canterbury; he always thought that
two less headstrong men than Thomas and King Henry
might have settled their differences by negotiation, and he
wanted to keep some room for manœuvre, without being
driven to take a stand on a point of principle from which
he could never retreat. He therefore gave public orders
that Thomas must not use his Legatine powers until

Easter 1166, which was April 24th. That was a warning to King Henry that he had eighteen months to reach an agreement with a friendly Pope, before he faced the thunders of an extremely unfriendly Legate.

If Thomas lived in the Papal household while these negotiations took place Henry might legitimately complain that his adversary had the private ear of the judge. So it was arranged that Thomas should lodge in the Cistercian Abbey of Pontigny. Alexander was, as usual, pressed for money, and the King of France offered an allowance for expenses; though apparently it was not enough and the Abbey was in fact out of pocket. But the Cistercians, traditionally Papalist, were proud that they had been chosen for the honour of sheltering an exiled Archbishop, and bore the cost willingly.

For the first time in his life Thomas, aged forty-six, was not busy all day. It was also the first time since he left Merton that he was exclusively in the company of monks. He wrote letters to his chief supporters to say how happy he was, attending all the offices in choir and filling the rest of his leisure with the study of Canon Law. But in fact it did not suit him. He was a warrior and a sportsman and a skilled administrator; now he had no riding and no work on his desk, and the study of Canon Law meant that he spent most of his time brooding over his grievances and thinking up further arguments against Henry, which was very bad for his temper. His theatrical sense of the fitting behaviour for a persecuted Confessor led him to live as a Cistercian monk, but broken sleep and a diet of bread and cabbage were too much for a digestion long accustomed to roast pheasant and a little of the very best wine. He fell seriously ill, and on doctor's orders went back to his nourishing dinners. Presently the Pope sent him a present of a grey Cistercian cowl, specially blessed, and he took to wearing it over the black Augustinian gown which he wore over his secular dress; since the stiff hair-shirt was underneath the lot he looked very bulky, and some people thought he had grown fat in the idleness of exile. It seems that this sudden attempt to take up in middle age the hard life of a Cistercian, after a youth of luxury and good living, permanently damaged his health. He always felt cold, even under the mountain of clothes he now wore; he was seldom free from indigestion, and that, with the chilblains and lassitude of a poor circulation, made him more irritable and quick-tempered than ever.

Even his supporters grew worried at his bad temper; it was evident that in his present state he would never make peace with the King. John of Salisbury wrote recommending the study of Theology rather than Canon Law as an occupation for his leisure, saying bluntly that if he meditated on the power and love of God he might eventually learn meekness. John of Poictiers raised another delicate issue; Thomas had always been fond of state; now the number of horses and servants he considered essential to his position were a great expense to his hosts; John suggested that if he wrote fewer letters abusing the King he would not need so many mounted messengers to carry them, and the Abbey of Pontigny would be the richer. Thomas agreed to both suggestions, for he was aware of his faults and anxious to correct them. But even while he endured the strain of bad health, anxiety and idleness, those who saw him daily were struck with admiration of his courage and energy.

Of course no one dared to tell King Henry to control

his temper. At his Christmas court of 1164 he gave full rein to his malignant spite. First he declared that Thomas had forfeited his Archbishopric by leaving the country without royal permission, and ordered Ranulf de Broc, a neighbouring landowner, to administer all the possessions of the See on behalf of the Crown. The forfeiture was justified by law, but a King bent on peace would have found another administrator, for the family of Broc were notorious as bad neighbours to all clerks; Ranulf exacted the uttermost farthing from the tenants, and particularly oppressed the monks of Christ Church by compelling them to accept unsuitable and loose-living friends of his as members of their wealthy community.

That was legal, though rigorous; but King Henry went much farther. Without any right in law he decreed that all members of the Becket family, and all landowners who had openly expressed sympathy for the Archbishop, must leave England for ever; and of course he seized their land for himself. As late as 1203 small yeomen, not in any way related to Thomas, were paying fines to King John to get back their own land. Before the penniless exiles crossed the Channel they were compelled to take oath that they would present themselves before the Archbishop, wherever he might be, that he might see the ruin he had brought on his friends and kin. We are told that four hundred of them came to the Abbey of Pontigny, and incidentally this episode gives us one of the few references to Thomas's sisters, who played little part in his life.

Luckily there was one prosperous part of Europe which always had a welcome for outlaws fleeing the wrath of the Duke of Normandy. The Kingdom of Sicily had been founded by Norman pilgrims who left home because they

were in trouble with the law, and they were glad of reinforcements to strengthen the dominant race against their
Greek, Italian, and Saracen subjects. The Norman Archbishop of Syracuse bore the expense of the journey, and
at the present day the widespread Italian family of Bec-
chetti claim descent from the kin of the Archbishop. (I
think myself they are mistaken; Thomas had no brothers,
and there is no reason why his cousins should have been
called Becket, the personal nickname of his father.)

Apart from these four hundred Thomas had no English
supporters in the spring of 1165. The general opinion was
expressed by the Augustinian William of Newburgh,
a contemporary historian who wrote that the Archbishop's
conduct issued from a laudable zeal to serve God and His
Church, but was not in itself praiseworthy, since his flight
served no useful purpose and only made the King more
angry than before. The rest of Christendom reproached
Henry as a persecutor, but he was delighted to find himself secure in his own Kingdom, which Stephen had lost
when he quarrelled with the Church. He decided to go
further, and bring pressure on the Pope by negotiating
with the Emperor.

At Pentecost (23rd May) 1165 a council assembled at
Wurzburg in Germany, where as many Bishops as could
be gathered were to swear obedience to the new Antipope
'Paschal III', who held Rome and was acknowledged in
most of the Empire. King Henry was represented, but
not by a Bishop; he did not intend to commit the sin of
schism, only to frighten the true Pope by appearing to be
about to commit it; he sent a delegation led by a royal
clerk, one John of Oxford, and their real object was to
negotiate a marriage between an English princess and the

Duke of Saxony. But John of Oxford, to please the Emperor, made some sort of conditional offer to recognize the Antipope. Later he denied having done anything of the kind, and of course if he did swear obedience without instructions that would not bind his master; but the rumour spread through England, and the King's vassals became seriously disturbed. It was one thing to be neutral in a quarrel between the King and Canterbury; such quarrels had been frequent ever since Anselm fled from William Rufus, and in fact good relations might be considered exceptional. It was quite another thing for England, which had always been famous for loyalty to the Holy See, to acknowledge a schismatic puppet of the Emperor; it might eventually lead to the Emperor claiming suzerainty over the Kingdom, and Henry would no longer be King by the Grace of God alone.

The magnates of England had already demonstrated their loyalty to the Pope. Shortly before the Council of Wurzburg the Emperor had sent the Archbishop of Cologne to open discussions on Princess Matilda's proposed marriage. This Archbishop was of course an Imperialist and a servant of the Antipope, and thus in the eyes of Papalists excommunicate. Though the King's council talked business with him, for the German marriage was important, the Earl of Leicester refused to greet him with the customary Kiss of Peace, and the altars at which he had said Mass were stripped of their ornaments and left desolate until they had been reconsecrated by a Bishop of the correct obedience. Alexander saw that Henry would be dethroned if he tried to lead his country into schism. The threat which should have been so frightening only strengthened the Pope's position, for it showed that Henry was not absolute master of his vassals. Of course in theory no feudal King should be absolute, though the King of England had greater power than most of his equals.

In November Pope Alexander was back in his palace of the Lateran in Rome, much stronger and less accessible to envoys from England. From time to time Henry still talked to his intimates about going over to the Antipope if Rome continued her support of the Archbishop; but everyone knew he dared not carry his threat into effect. The Pope could resume his efforts to make peace, secure that his authority would be recognized in England. The only result of the flirtation with the Emperor was that Henry had wasted most of the eighteen months of grace allowed him.

On Easter Sunday 1166 Thomas's full powers as Metropolitan and Legate in England were restored to him. The decree was actually pronounced in Rome, but everyone in England and France knew it was coming, and both sides had made their preparations in advance.

Everything now turned on the delivery of legal documents. A Bishop could not be suspended until the sentence, sealed in due form by his legal superior, had been actually placed in his hands, or at least read out from the altar of his Cathedral. If he was sentenced he might appeal to Rome, and the sentence would be in abeyance until the appeal was decided; or he might appeal in advance, and prevent the sentence ever being published; but to do that he must serve notice on the person of his adversary, and volunteer a definite date in the reasonably near future when his lawyers would be ready to open their case in Rome. It was a great advantage to have your documents properly served while your adversary's messengers were still riding about the countryside, and all parties made use of the rather childish subterfuge of being missing from their customary haunts, leaving no forwarding address.

The King knew Thomas could do nothing until he had received a document which had been sealed in Rome on Easter Sunday. His advisers drew up a protest in very wide terms, appealing to the Pope against anything the Archbishop might do; but of course this appeal would be meaningless if it was served on Thomas before he had received his powers, for you cannot appeal against what a man may not lawfully do. He must be served in the short interval while he possessed Legatine authority but had not yet made use of it, a ticklish problem of timing. The King's clerks did their best, and messengers rode to Pontigny shortly after Easter, with instructions to watch the roads for the Papal couriers and follow immediately with the appeal. But something went wrong, and when they rode up to the Abbey they discovered that the Archbishop of Canterbury had set out on pilgrimage, no one knew whither.

Thomas actually went to Soissons, where there was a shrine of little interest to the average Archbishop, but for which he had a special reverence. St. Drausius is one of the more obscure saints, but French knights accused of felony had discovered by experience that they stood a better chance of winning the duel by which their guilt was decided if they prayed by his tomb on the night before the battle. Thomas spent the night in vigil beside the tomb, as though he were actually to cross lances with King Henry. In times of stress the knight would come before the Archbishop in his many-sided character.

From Soissons he travelled to Vézelay, a famous church

which contained the relics of St. Mary Magdalen; great crowds assembled there annually for the Feast of Pentecost, and on Whit Sunday the 12th of June 1166 the Archbishop of Canterbury made use of his new powers to pronounce sentence on his enemies before such a large audience. First he excommunicated Ranulf de Broc, and all who unjustly detained the revenues of the See of Canterbury; that was common form, and the Brocs must have known that they automatically excommunicated themselves the moment they began to farm Church lands. Then he excommunicated John of Oxford and Richard of Ilchester, the royal clerks who were alleged to have sworn obedience to the Antipope at Wurzburg; that also was to be expected. But then he suspended from his episcopal functions Bishop Jocelyn of Salisbury, a sound Papalist who had stood by him at Northampton. Jocelyn had appointed John of Oxford to the Deanery of Salisbury. John was a royal clerk, and such appointments were the recognized way of rewarding useful officials; but Jocelyn had known that he lay under suspicion of schism, and had been directly ordered by his exiled Archbishop not to admit him. Driven to choose between King and Church, Bishop Jocelyn had weakly appointed the schismatic, hoping that his good record at Northampton would save him from punishment. This suspension was public notice that there was no room for neutrals in the struggle which impended. Every Bishop must choose between obedience to the King and obedience to the Pope; it was Henry's weakness that even those churchmen who thought the King was in the right could not bring themselves to disobey the Holy See, though they argued and appealed at great length before finally submitting.

Thomas also excommunicated, without mentioning names, those who profited by the benefices unjustly taken from his supporters. This was aimed at, and hit, Gilbert Foliot of London, who had been charged by the King to administer these vacant livings. Gilbert was honest in financial matters, and inquired from the Pope what he should do with the money; Alexander ordered him to send it oversea to its rightful owners, but the King forbade, and Gilbert kept it in a special account until peace should be made. As a Cluniac monk he was unswervingly loyal to the Pope, but he had always disliked and despised Thomas. During the whole quarrel he endured great mental anguish, pulled one way by personal and political sentiments, and the other by his vow of obedience. But as the most reputable of the Archbishop's foes he did Thomas a great deal of harm.

Then the congregation waited for the thrill of hearing Thomas excommunicate his King and release the vassals of England from their allegiance. But there were no more sentences. Thomas had heard that Henry lay dangerously ill, and it was rumoured that he was dying. It is strong proof that he still loved the comrade of his youth that at this juncture he held his hand. If Henry died excommunicate he would go straight to Hell, and that punishment was too much, even to save the liberty of the Church. Thomas went quietly back to Pontigny, leaving the King unharmed.

Bishop Jocelyn was deeply grieved at his suspension. At Northampton he had pledged the possessions of his See to buy Henry's goodwill, and he had put up bail, which had been forfeited, that the Archbishop would stand to judgement. Nevertheless he submitted loyally. But Gilbert

of London was more stubborn. Besides his personal dislike of Thomas as a man he was coming to reject the
authority of any Archbishop of Canterbury. England
was a land of few dioceses, and it was unusual that such
a great Kingdom should be divided into only two Provinces; in the past there had been schemes to divide the
vast Province of Canterbury by elevating Winchester
into another Archbishopric for the south-west. But about
this time Geoffrey of Monmouth's astonishing romance
was becoming widely known, and Geoffrey described the
south of England in King Arthur's day as being under the
ecclesiastical rule of an Archbishop of *London* (which may
be true of late Roman times). A title dating from the
fifth century appealed to the twelfth, so busy in restoring
what it thought to be the civilization of the great days of
Rome. When Gilbert was translated from Hereford to
London he had refused the canonical oath of obedience to
Thomas. His excuse was that he had already sworn obedience to Archbishop Theobald at his consecration, and
that such an oath was binding for life and need not be
repeated; because everyone knew that the two men were
on bad terms personally this excuse had been tactfully
allowed. He now took advantage of the concession to
begin putting out propaganda that the See of London
should by rights come directly under the Pope. He further announced that he appealed against everything
Thomas had done at Vezelay, and gave notice that his
lawyers would be in Rome ready to argue the case by
next Easter.

At this rate the quarrel would never be settled, though
everyone except Thomas and Henry was eager for peace.
Pope Alexander in particular longed for a settlement, for

the Emperor was marching south, and it looked as though he would soon be driven from Rome once more. The Archbishop had proved that he could be a serious menace, since English Bishops obeyed his sentences without defiance; while Henry's counter-threat to make terms with the Antipope was more than his vassals would permit him to carry out. But meanwhile Henry, with the personal spite which he displayed from first to last, had intervened to drive Thomas into the arms of the King of France; who had hitherto done nothing more than hover in the background and suggest that two such gallant knights ought to meet in a meadow and be friends again. The Cistercians, unlike some religious orders, had a central organization, and representatives of all their monasteries met once a year at the mother-house of Citeaux. The King of England sent letters to this General Chapter threatening that if Pontigny continued to harbour his enemy he would pillage the Cistercian houses in England. This threat to the great foundations of Waverley, Rievaulx, and Fountains was too serious to be disregarded; the Abbot of Pontigny informed Thomas that though of course no monk could drive away a fugitive it would certainly be more convenient if he chose another place of exile. When King Louis heard of it he sent for the Archbishop and offered him a home in the royal Abbey of St. Colombe near Sens, for as long as he should wish to remain.

On the 11th of November 1166 Thomas moved to St. Colombe, after nearly two years at Pontigny. He had now more or less adjusted himself to exile, filling his days with prayer, and with study of the procedure of Canon Law; he missed the hard work of administration that used to keep him busy, and his driving energy had to be satisfied with finding the most stringent methods of passing sentence on his suffragans, so that the inevitable appeal to Rome should be as difficult as possible. But soon after he reached Sens he received letters from the Pope, informing him that his Legatine and Metropolitan powers were withdrawn until further notice, and that Alexander had remitted all the sentences passed at Vezelay. The Pope made it clear that he regarded the sentences as lawful and just, and that he remitted them only as an act of clemency. But it was a severe snub, and what was even more trying, Thomas now found himself with nothing to do.

CHAPTER TEN

NEGOTIATIONS AND INTERVIEWS

Everyone was back where he had been two years ago, and it was time to negotiate a peace, without victory to either side. Pope Alexander appointed a commission of two Cardinals to mediate between Archbishop and King. That they were mediators, not judges, is shown by their instructions; they were forbidden to enter England, and thus to inquire into the workings of the Constitutions of Clarendon, until they had reconciled Thomas and Henry; and to show that he sought compromise, not victory for the Church, the Pope joined in the commission Cardinal Otho, a supporter of Thomas, with Cardinal William of Pavia, who disliked the Archbishop and considered he was in the wrong.

The reason, of course, why the Pope was so anxious to regain the friendship of the King of England was that the Emperor seemed to be winning the war. But during the next year Italy saw rapid changes of fortune, and meanwhile military operations delayed the arrival of the Legates. They were appointed in December 1166, in Rome; but all the passes over the Alps were in the hands of the Ghibellines; they took eleven months for the journey, and did not reach Sens until November 1167, when the situation had changed. In April 1167 Alexander fled southwards from Rome, and in August the Antipope 'Paschal

III' was solemnly enthroned in the Lateran; but in September pestilence raged in the German army which had brought him; the soldiers died by thousands, and the frightened survivors fled over the Alps. The Pope returned to his lawful See, stronger than ever after this manifest intervention of Heaven in the affairs of earth. It was no longer quite so important to keep the support of the King of England.

During this latter part of his exile, while he was living in the Abbey of St. Colombe, Thomas was as obstinate as a mule and as slippery as an eel. Since everyone told him that peace was the great essential he continually offered to make peace as suggested; but only on his own terms, after Henry had surrendered every point in dispute. The mediators, like all mediators in every age, wasted their efforts in trying to find an ambiguous formula which might be differently interpreted by each party, so that each would think he had gained the victory. But both King and Archbishop were keen lawyers, and both spotted at once that the harmless little clause which his opponent wished to add, and which the mediators considered nothing more than a gesture, in fact gave away the whole case.

The Cardinals first conferred with Thomas at Sens, and persuaded him to promise he would swear obedience to his King, 'saving the rights of God and of his order'; that was a harmless oath which Bishops were willing to take in any Christian realm. Their aim was to get the King to receive his Archbishop in friendship, and after mutual oaths and the exchange of the solemn Kiss of Peace Thomas would go back to Canterbury. Nothing was said about the Constitutions of Clarendon; the Pope could not

St. Thomas of Canterbury, Archbishop and Martyr

From a mosaic in the church of Monreale in Sicily. Joan
daughter of King Henry II married King William of Sicily
in 1177, and this mosaic was designed *c.* 1190. Therefore it
was meant to be seen by people who had known Thomas
when he was alive, and is probably the best portrait that
has come down to us

openly approve them, or compel a clerk to swear they were lawful; but obviously they would continue in force; the Archbishop might protest against them, and his protest would be disregarded. Of course Thomas and Henry must not meet until they had learned perfectly the parts they would play at the solemn reconciliation, for everyone knew they irritated one another. The Cardinals rode off hopefully to Gisors on the border of Normandy, where Henry was holding a conference with Louis of France about the everlasting problem of the Vexin.

The Cardinals spoke with the King in a little solar, and no record survives of what was said. But evidently they offended Henry's quick temper. Presently they came out, very red in the face, and rode off to their lodging with unusual haste. Henry escorted them to his outer gate, as courtesy demanded, and was overheard to say as he turned back, 'I hope to God I never set eyes on another Cardinal!' The projected interview did not take place.

The year 1168 was wasted in tentative efforts to get the parties to agree at long range without meeting. The Pope was growing tired of Thomas and his unyielding firmness; an unofficial suggestion came from the Lateran that if the King would abolish his unlawful Constitutions Alexander would certainly translate Thomas to some See at present in infidel hands, where he would never again be a nuisance to Christian Kings. That would have been the most hopeful arrangement for future peace; but the King was set on his Constitutions, and he refused.

Meanwhile the Church in England was suffering from the absence of its head. Ranulf de Broc was oppressing the tenants of Canterbury, and there was serious danger that the lands of the See might be permanently alienated. In the twelfth century custom grew quickly; the legal maxim was that 'three times makes a custom', and if any vassal rendered the same service for three years in succession his heirs might be charged with it to the end of time. Ranulf might introduce unauthorized services which would never be shaken off.

Besides these material worries there were the normal disputes between diocesan Bishops, or between Abbots and the Bishops within whose Sees their Abbeys were situated, which in ordinary times would be settled by the Metropolitan. Now there was no way of settling them, for of course no Bishop, however much he hated Thomas, would be so disloyal to his order as to bring purely ecclesiastical disputes before the King. The Abbot of St. Augustines in Canterbury itself was trying to get his house exempted from episcopal control; one of his arguments was that the Archbishop had not visited the community for years, and there was no prospect that he would visit it in the foreseeable future. Monks were being admitted to Christ Church without being made to take the necessary oath of obedience to their Abbot *ex officio*; the Prior of Christ Church wrote offering to stop this irregularity if Thomas commanded, but pointing out that in that case the daily office, the chief work for which the great Cathedral had been built, would come to a stop for lack of new monks. The Bishop of London was trying to get himself made the third Archbishop in England, and if he succeeded other Bishops would copy his example. It was the fear that unless peace was made England would be divided into a dozen independent Sees, each Bishop excommunicating his colleagues for default of obedience, that was the strongest force urging Thomas to surrender.

He might have tried to keep order with a few long-range excommunications of his own, but in May 1168 the Pope, fearing his fiery temper, forbade him to take any disciplinary action until Easter 1169. This was lucky for the Bishop of London. Thomas, to test whether he still obeyed his canonical superior, had ordered him to come to Sens. Gilbert resented the order, and at once sent notice that he appealed to the Pope against it; he was always sending these notices of appeal, which had the effect of delaying the penalties of disobedience; then, after he had procured as many adjournments as he could, and spun out matters with all the procrastination of a medieval lawsuit, he would finally instruct his lawyers to submit to judgement without arguing the merits of the case. But though he was a King's man and an enemy of Canterbury, he had been trained at Cluny; when he received a formal order from his lawful superior he would protest and delay and try to wriggle out of it, but he could not bring himself to commit the sin of open disobedience. He began to ride slowly towards Southampton. In Southampton he was looking, not very diligently, for a ship to take him to France when he heard that Thomas's powers had been revoked; which he interpreted, rather liberally, as a licence to disobey him. He returned in triumph to London.

The Pope also revoked the Legatine commission he had given to the two Cardinals, and appointed instead a commission of two learned theologians. This was an acknowledgment that conciliation and appeasement were useless with such legal sticklers as Henry and Thomas; it was no good commanding them to kiss and be friends;

they would not be content with less than a formal judgement of every point in dispute.

All this time good King Louis was plugging away at his simple idea that if the two old comrades in arms could only meet face to face their friendship would revive. At last, after a certain amount of misrepresentation to each principal of his antagonist's alleged willingness to give way, a meeting was arranged for the Feast of the Epiphany, the 6th of January 1169, at Montmirail in Henry's county of Maine. King Louis and the new Papal Legates were also present, to sanction any agreement which might be reached. The supporters of both sides rode with high hopes to the meeting, for everyone except the two leaders was heartily sick of the quarrel.

First the two Kings met, for they had to ratify yet another treaty about the Vexin. They rode together, and exchanged the Kiss of Peace. This was a peculiarly solemn way of demonstrating an intention to be friends in the future, though what exactly it implied is rather hard to say. King Henry attached great importance to the ceremony, and would not grant the Kiss unless he really intended peace, as we shall see; and the Earl of Leicester would not exchange it with a schismatic. But the only other example of its employment as a serious pledge of peace that I can call to mind is when Robert Bruce exchanged it with the Red Comyn; since immediately afterwards Bruce murdered his rival before the altar where both had received Communion, the Kiss might not in all circumstances be a sure sign of amity.

Soon afterwards Thomas rode up with his escort of faithful clerks. When he saw Henry, whom he had not met since Northampton, he was actually overcome by memories of their old friendship, as King Louis had hoped. He dismounted and knelt before his lord, and Henry, equally affectionate, dismounted and held the stirrup for his spiritual father to mount. But then they came to business, and the old rancour flared up. Henry had let it be known unofficially that if Thomas made formal submission the Constitutions would not in fact be strictly enforced; and he had been led to believe that Thomas had agreed in advance to this compromise. Such are the perils of permitting well-meaning third parties to attempt to reconcile adversaries without settling the matter in dispute. But Thomas, though he knew of Henry's offer, would not credit the King's bare word without a seal to back it. He knew Henry very well indeed, and he may have been right to distrust him. When it was time for Thomas to make submission he knelt dutifully and repeated the formula, but he added the fatal clause, 'saving the honour of God, and the rights of Holy Church, and the rights of my order'.

Henry was furious. He turned to King Louis and shouted a long tirade: 'See how foolishly and proudly this man deserted his church! For he ran away by night, though neither I nor anyone else drove him out of the Kingdom. Now he persuades you that his is the cause of the Church, and that he suffers for justice' sake, and thus he has deceived many great people. I asked for nothing from the Archbishop but that he should keep those customs which his five immediate predecessors (of whom some are Saints, famed for miracles) all observed to mine, and to which he himself has assented; let him pledge himself to keep them, without any subterfuge. The sole cause of dissension between us is that he infringes them, and that at Vezelay, that famous place, on a high festival, he condemned some of them and excommunicated those who observed them!'

That was a very persuasive exposition of the King's standpoint; it was quite true that every King since the Conquest had done what Henry claimed the right to do, and that every Archbishop of Canterbury, including St. Anselm who was already canonized, had sometimes submitted to the royal command. But previous Kings, though they might forbid a particular appeal to Rome, had never announced that there would be no more appeals without the King's leave, or tried to get an Archbishop to swear in public that he would observe a code of customs which were contrary to Canon Law; and in fact there had been sufficient resistance to maintain the rights of the Church; St. Anselm had gone into exile, exactly like Thomas, rather than submit to Rufus.

But the general sense of the meeting was on Henry's side. Thomas's own clerks begged their lord to submit, and even King Louis at last turned against him. Seeing him still obstinate the two Kings rode off in anger, without taking the formal leave which politeness demanded. Some of their courtiers lingered to reproach the Archbishop for his stubborness, and the only hopeful sign at this disappointing interview was that he bore their anger meekly, without answering as once he would have answered; that seemed to show he was anxious for peace, if it could be had on terms that satisfied his conscience. More than four years of exile had taught him to control his temper.

As the exiles rode back to Sens they discussed the question of where they would find shelter in the future, for it seemed likely that King Louis would no longer support such a stubborn enemy of Kings. They spoke loudly, so that Thomas might hear and understand that he had lost the good opinion of a chivalrous knight and King who saw the dispute impartially. One, Henry of Houghton, even tried the effect of ridicule; his horse stumbled, and as he jerked at the bit he rebuked horse and Archbishop together: 'Will you obey my command to pick up your feet, of course saving the honour of God and the rights of Holy Church and of your order?' Thomas still kept his temper, which was almost as surprising as if he had given in to the King. But his notorious saving clause became a popular catchword, added as a joke to every order to a servant.

Thomas must have been very near despair; it never occurred to him that he might be in the wrong, or that the matter in dispute was unimportant and a fit subject for compromise; he knew that unhindered intercourse with Rome was vital to the unity and discipline of the English Church. But nobody else seemed to understand its importance. The Pope could not openly abandon his faithful servant who had gone into exile to uphold the integrity of Canon Law, but he was obviously attempting to arrange some compromise which would in fact leave the King supreme; it was whispered unofficially that he was heartily tired of this stubborn supporter who would not surrender when he was beaten. The King of France, who represented the opinion of the best type of gallant, chivalrous, thick-headed knight, was turning against the exile who had lived so long on his bounty. Even the faithful clerks who had left rich benefices in England to share their lord's perils were beginning to remember they were Anglo-Normans (their names show they were not Saxon), and that if they could not overcome the obstinacy of their leader they would never see home again. He was alone, faced with the hostility of the King and the unfriendly neutrality of the clergy and chivalry of Christendom.

But as he crossed the border from Maine to the Ile de France he realized that he was not alone. News of the conference had spread through the countryside faster than a horse could travel, and the common people were firm in support of the Church which was their only ally against the greed and oppression of their lords. Peasants lined the roadside, kneeling for his blessing, and as he passed they called after him: 'There goes the Archbishop who would not deny God or neglect His honour, even at the command of two Kings.'

The Kings rode away in company, to continue the negotiations for a firm peace between France and Normandy. But the more Louis saw of Henry the more he realized there was something to be said for Thomas, for Henry's arbitrary rage and cruelty made him obviously unfit to control the relations of Church and State; Louis also knew, as every King of France knew in his heart, that he would never put down the pride of his great vassals unless he kept the affection of the common people; he was impressed when he heard that the Archbishop had ridden back to Sens by roads thronged with peasants. At the close of the conference he went out of his way to visit Sens, summoned the Archbishop to the castle, and knelt before him, confessing that at Montmirail he had considered Henry to be in the right and had planned to expel the refugees; but now he had come to his senses and he thought Thomas so wholly justified that he regarded his earlier doubts as a sin, for which he begged absolution. The Abbey of St. Colombe would continue to shelter the Archbishop, and on Palm Sunday the Pope's suspension of his powers would be ended; Thomas could take up once more the stubborn struggle.

He therefore rode to celebrate Easter at the monastery of Clairvaux, which St. Bernard had made the most famous in Christendom; for he knew that at that season it would be crowded and his sentences would receive full publicity. At the earliest opportunity, the High Mass of Palm Sunday the 13th of April 1169, he excommunicated Bishop Gilbert of London for disobedience in administering the See of Canterbury while the lawful occupant was in exile, and gave public notice that on Ascension Day, the 29th of May, he would excommunicate anyone who in spite of this warning still farmed the endowments of Canterbury sacrilegiously for the King's benefit.

Gilbert Foliot had early news of his excommunication, and it never occurred to his highly-disciplined Cluniac conscience to defy it. But he remained determined to stick to the side which he thought was in the right. He sought refuge in the quibble that the sentence would not take effect until it had been served on him personally or read aloud from the high altar of his Cathedral; he therefore went into hiding and continued to celebrate Mass as though he were not under the ban, while the King's servants watched the ports to intercept the messenger who carried the formal deed of excommunication.

If the King could prevent the publication of Papal documents in England he would in fact be master of the English Church, and Thomas made a special effort to see his sentence published in the most striking manner possible. He very rarely permitted his followers to run into any danger which he did not share himself, but on this occasion he accepted the offer of two gallant laymen who were eager to serve the Church in defiance of King Henry's rage. William and Berengar smuggled the deed into England, for the King's officers, thinking it would be carried by a clerk, did not search laymen carefully. But when they inquired for Bishop Gilbert no one could say where he was to be found, and their only course was the very dangerous one of presenting it to be read aloud in St. Paul's Cathedral in London.

They chose their opportunity with care. Ascension Day was then, as it still is, a Holiday of Obligation, that is, a day when all the faithful are required to attend at Mass at least once. The burgesses of London, more devout then than nowadays, were accustomed on great feast days to receive Communion at an early Mass; later they would drop into St. Paul's to pass the holiday morning in listening to the chanting of the choir at High Mass and the preacher's exhortations; but since they had performed their obligation before breakfast they would leave immediately after the sermon. The messengers went in plenty of time for the High Mass, and when the sermon ended they were standing in the front row of the crowd (in the twelfth century the only seats in a church were the choir stalls in the chancel; the lay congregation always stood). The well-endowed Church of those happy times was not compelled to pass round the plate at every opportunity, and at this Mass there was no general collection; but immediately after the sermon comes the Offertory, in which the priest offers to God the bread and wine which he will shortly consecrate; and if anyone intended to make a gift to God, of his own free will or in fulfilment of a vow, this was the appropriate time to bring it to the altar-rail. William approached with his imposing parchment, the seal dangling; the priest came joyfully down to receive it, thinking that here were the title-deeds to another manor for the upkeep of the Cathedral. But when the deed was safely delivered Berengar seized hold of the celebrant, and commanded him, by the obedience he owed to Rome, not to continue the Mass until he had read it aloud from the steps of the altar. The priest recited it, and Gilbert of London was now excommunicate; for sentence had been pronounced before his vacant throne in his own Cathedral.

I am glad to say the two brave laymen got away safely. The congregation, who had only come to hear the sermon, at once pushed through the great west door to spread this exciting news in the city; the fugitives mingled with the surging throng and escaped unnoticed. Probably a burgess hid them, but many considered their escape was miraculous.

The only churchman who was not delighted with this stirring defiance was the Pope himself. His war with the Emperor was at last going well, and the cities of Lombardy were making head against the German army. A treaty had been proposed by which King Henry was to send them 6,000 marks in cash, and what armed assistance he could spare; in return they would proclaim him King of independent Lombardy, no longer a part of the Holy Roman Empire. Nothing came of this proposal; it is doubtful whether King Henry, or anyone else living at that time, ever possessed 6,000 marks, 960,000 silver pennies, all at once; and after he had protected his wide-flung frontiers, from the Cheviots to the Pyrenees, he never had the knights to form an army of invasion. But for another hundred years the mirage of a realm in Italy haunted every King of England, until Henry III ruined his finances in the effort to make his son Edmund King of Sicily. The Pope now saw that his impetuous supporter in the case of Canon Law would lose him the help of his most valuable ally on the battlefield. He reacted as soon as the news reached him. Ascension Day was the 29th of May, and on the 19th of June, at Benevento in southern Italy, Alexander solemnly absolved all those whom Thomas had excommunicated, and forbade him to inflict any further punishment until after the Feast of the Assumption, the 15th of August.

Meanwhile Bishop Gilbert, who was never happy in this unfortunate quarrel with his canonical superior (though he was much too certain that his side was right to dream of giving way), had set out to receive absolution from the only source which can remove the ban of a Metropolitan Archbishop, the Papacy. He could travel fast when he wished, and he was in Milan before he learned that the Archbishop of Rouen had received a Legatine commission to absolve him. He was soon back in London, ruling his See competently as though nothing had happened. But he had been made to look very foolish, especially by his pointless scurry over the Alps, and in future he, the most respectable of Thomas's opponents, did not carry so much weight with the opinion of educated Europe.

Pope Alexander had fixed the time-limit of the Assumption because he hoped that by then his new Legates would have arranged terms of peace. Actually, with the difficulty of travel through war-torn Italy and the notorious slackness in journeying of all temporary Legates, who relished the deference which was their due in every monastery they visited, the envoys did not reach King Henry, at Argentan in Normandy, until early August. Vivian, archdeacon of Orvieto and Gratian, the notary, were not eminent men come to preach peace, certain of a hearing because of their greatness, like the two Cardinals who had been so rudely rebuffed at Gisors; they were highly skilled lawyers of no social importance, and their task was to draw up a formula which both sides might accept. If they could also settle the question of appeals to Rome so much the better, but in any case clever lawyers should be able to compose an oath of submission which Thomas would be willing to tender and Henry to receive.

Pope Alexander had reckoned without the immovable obstinacy of the two disputants. Thomas was willing to swear submission if he might add the words 'saving the honour of God and the rights of my order'. After a great deal of haggling Henry said this would content him, if he might reply that he accepted the Archbishop's submission 'saving the dignity of the Kingdom of England'. That meant that the Constitutions of Clarendon would remain in force, though the Archbishop would be spared the disgrace of acknowledging them on oath. Thomas refused this compromise. Then Henry, who was at last beginning to tire of the interminable argument, offered to restore the lands of Canterbury; there would be no oath of submission, and the Archbishop might continue to live in France if he preferred it; but he would live there as a very wealthy man, not openly hostile to the King of England;

and to demonstrate his goodwill he would promise not to excommunicate any subject of the King.

It was a tempting offer, and his followers put great pressure on Thomas to accept. By now it was obvious to everyone that the quarrel would not end until one of the parties was dead, but this compromise would allow innocent bystanders to live in peace and get on with the administration of the English Church, which must be administered by someone or it would fall to pieces for lack of a head. The exiles were anxious to go home and resume their forfeited benefices. But Thomas, after some hesitation, saw that the King was really bribing him to give way, which was indeed the truth. He refused any terms except withdrawal of the Constitutions, and to show he was in earnest announced that if the King was still recalcitrant, in six months' time, on Candlemas the 2nd of February 1170, all England would be placed under Interdict.

On the 8th of September, after four weeks of fruitless argument, the Legates abandoned hope of success and began their return journey to Italy.

Henry was seriously alarmed at the threat of an Interdict, the most solemn punishment the Church could inflict on his subjects. In an interdicted land religious life came almost to a stop; in each church there was only one very low Mass on Sundays and holidays, none at all on ordinary days of the week; only the dying might receive Communion; and weddings, baptisms and funerals were reduced to their bare essentials and held in the open air. In the twelfth century most laymen were sufficiently devout to find this a considerable deprivation, and even the indifferent would miss the choral singing and processions which in those days took the place of the modern concert hall and theatre. Worst of all, from Henry's point of view, public opinion would consider rebellion justified. The King of France might even take the opportunity to declare Normandy and Aquitaine forfeited from an unchristian Duke, which in fact was one of the excuses used by King Philip Augustus against King John in the next generation. Henry at once sent envoys to the Pope, hoping to persuade him to withdraw the Archbishop's powers. But he also took precautions in his own realm.

He did not think it necessary to visit England. His French duchies and counties were more important than his Kingdom, and France was the centre of Christendom, where the political issues of the western world were decided. But he sent orders that all his free tenants must at once take oath before his sheriffs that they would not obey any Papal commands which might be published without his permission. (Papal commands, not Archiepiscopal, because only in his capacity of Papal Legate could Thomas declare an Interdict.) This was a tremendous undertaking, comparable in the amount of work it gave to his servants to the compiling of Domesday Book ninety years before, and it is interesting to see what the people of England made of it; for it is not easy to find out what they thought at the time of this quarrel between two Frenchmen who had lived in France for the last five years.

Most laymen took the oath, though some added reservations which deprived it of all meaning. Many of those who refused, like the Countess (in her own right) of Devon, were magnates who thought themselves immune from royal vengeance by the greatness of their social position. But the clergy were more difficult to persuade. Gilbert of London, the only Bishop who might have sworn willingly, happened to be out of the country, still returning from his hasty visit to Milan. Roger of York, though he hated Thomas, openly refused to swear. The mighty Henry of Winchester not only refused, but went out of his way to renew in public his oath of canonical obedience to Canterbury and Rome. Others were more timid; they did not refuse openly, but they could not be found when it was time to take the oath. The Bishop of Lichfield, whose diocese included the northern March, vanished among the Welsh mountains, leaving no address. The Bishops of Salisbury and Norwich, the latter a promoted monk never happy in the secular world, suddenly felt an urge to make lengthy retreats in strict monasteries, where neither sheriffs nor royal messengers were allowed past the gate. It was obvious that the Church as a whole, even those clerks who thought Thomas was in the wrong, would obey any orders he might issue.

Thomas waited until the King's government had gone to infinite trouble to receive a great many oaths, and then made nonsense of the whole affair. He published a decree absolving all the subjects of his Legation (and he was Legate for all England, not merely for Canterbury) from any oath they might have taken through fear of the King's servants. That absolved anyone who wished to be released; those who had taken the oath willingly, not from fear of royal displeasure, were on the King's side anyway, and their oaths were unnecessary.

Henry decided it was time to make peace. He could not afford to give the disaffected among his vassals the splendid war-cry that they were fighting for the rights of the

Church. But he still would not give up the Constitutions; he would merely make friends with his Archbishop and get him back to England; how they would live together afterwards could be decided as they came to try it. His own opinion of the future is pretty clear; about this time he remarked that England was not a bush big enough to shelter two such birds as Henry and Thomas. He *must* have expected that the Archbishop would die fairly soon, though he was not yet fifty-one.

The agreement must be reached before Candlemas, and since it was now November there was no time to be lost. Thomas let it be known that he would only meet his lord on French soil, with the King of France present to guarantee his safety; for apparently it was widely rumoured that he would suffer a fatal accident if he passed into Henry's power. Henry therefore sent envoys to Louis, ostensibly to treat of other matters, actually to hint that an invitation to the Ile de France would be very acceptable. But Louis did not care for his company, and the invitation was not issued. Henry brought matters to a head by setting out, uninvited, on a pilgrimage to the shrine of St. Denys, the martyred Bishop who was patron of the city of Paris. Out of ordinary politeness King Louis must go to Paris to receive him, and his love of peace-making, with his pathetic belief in the magic of a personal interview, made him ask Thomas to come with him. On the 18th of November the two Kings and the Archbishop met on the open hill of Montmartre, the Mount of the Martyr.

There was first a lengthy discussion about the restitution of the endowments of Canterbury and compensation for the exiles whose benefices had been seized by the King; both Henry and Thomas were keen men of business

who were determined to get every penny of their full
financial rights. But nothing whatever was said about the
Constitutions, the punishment of felonious clerks, or the
right of appeal to the Holy See. Probably Thomas had
at last come to realize that the Pope would be best served
if he gave way for the moment; Rome never abandons
a claim, and one day some future King would concede
the full liberty of the Church; but the important thing,
in the year 1169, was to keep Henry's support for Alexander III in his struggle with the Emperor.

At length Thomas dismounted, and standing before the
King promised to serve him as a loyal baron for the lands
of Canterbury and as a faithful friend in his spiritual capacity of Archbishop. It was not exactly the vassal's oath of
homage, which it was simony for a Bishop to swear to a
temporal ruler; but the promise had much the same effect.
He then waited for Henry to dismount in his turn, and by
giving the Kiss of Peace admit his Bishop and baron to
the royal protection and friendship. But Henry would not
grant the Kiss.

He tried to hedge. He explained that years ago in a fit
of rage he had sworn a great oath never to grant the Kiss
to this bitter enemy; his conscience would not allow him
to break this oath, but he promised that he would conduct
himself as a friend and protector, exactly as though he
had in fact kissed him.

This was nonsense, and the whole conference knew it.
Henry was always swearing horrible oaths about what he
would do to his enemies if ever they fell into his power; a
man who is so overmastered by insane rage that he wallows
naked on the floor and chews up his bedding cannot be
bound in his lucid intervals by what he swore in the heat

of anger; if his battered and maltreated conscience was the only thing that held him back the remedy was at hand; the Legate and Metropolitan had recently released the whole population of England from an unlawful oath, and he was fully empowered to absolve the King from a vow which was in itself sinful. But even after this had been pointed out to him Henry stuck to his refusal.

He was quibbling over a meaningless form, and his opponent was entitled to meet him on the same ground. But there was more in it than that. Since he was willing to promise friendship but not to grant the Kiss of Peace it was legitimate to infer that he had a superstitious reverence for the actual Kiss, and no reverence at all for his plighted word. Thomas could deduce two important facts: that the King was still secretly his foe, but that if he could be persuaded to grant the Kiss he would consider himself bound by it.

Thomas therefore withdrew the promise he had just made, explaining that it had been part of a bargain by which two enemies took mutual oaths of friendship. Since the King would not carry out his part of the deal the offer was no longer valid. King Louis agreed that this was fair and reasonable, and his approval meant the approval of every chivalrous knight in Christendom. The King of France escorted the Archbishop back to Paris, leaving Henry, very angry, sitting his horse on the hill of Montmartre.

By midnight Henry was even more angry. It had been assumed that this meeting would end in a reconciliation, and Louis had prepared a grand feast in Paris to celebrate the peace. Now he rode away without inviting the stubborn King of England, who was only in his dominions as a pilgrim to St. Denys, not as his guest. But Henry had counted on an invitation, and had made no arrangements for supper; he was thirty-six miles from his nearest castle, and the showy war-horse he rode for a ceremonial royal interview was not the mount he would have chosen for a long ride over bad roads in the dark. By the time he reached Mantes and his supper he was swearing and cursing terribly.

CHAPTER ELEVEN

THE CORONATION OF THE
YOUNG KING

Since peace had been so nearly made at Montmartre and it was hoped that King Henry would soon ratify his promise with the ritual Kiss, the Pope intervened to cancel the threatened Interdict. His instructions did not arrive until the middle of February 1170, but Thomas knew they were on the way and held his hand. About the same time the Pope wrote to King Henry, reminding him in a friendly way that it was the privilege of the Archbishop of Canterbury, and of him alone, to crown a King of England in Westminster Abbey.

In the twelfth century great men were supposed to consult their counsellors on every important matter, and to talk things over very thoroughly before they made an important decision. It was one of the accusations against Thomas that he made up his own mind and kept his plans for the future secret even from his companions. King Henry was more conventional, though the discussion seldom changed his opinion; but one result was that his future intentions usually leaked out in advance. It seems that in February the Pope had heard gossip about an impending Coronation in England.

That did not mean that King Henry expected to die, or planned to abdicate. But he remembered that a disputed succession had brought nearly twenty years of civil war to Stephen's Kingdom, and he genuinely sought order in his realm, even after he was gone; posterity has much admired this love of order, forgetting that it was achieved at the expense of justice and liberty. He wished to see his successor crowned in his lifetime, that the King's Peace might not be interrupted at his death.

In the twelfth century when the King died the throne was vacant until another King had been crowned. For this reason there was no interval for Court Mourning; when Rufus was killed Henry I rode hard to Westminster and was crowned immediately he arrived. But the question of who should succeed a dead monarch was not settled in advance, as it is nowadays. William the Conqueror succeeded because Edward the Confessor had left the Kingdom to him by will (or at least that was what he told his supporters); if that was correct the crown was not hereditary and a King might nominate any successor he chose. But the great lords also claimed the right to choose their future ruler, or at least to decide between two candidates who were both members of the royal family. No King since the Conquest had been the heir of his predecessor, by the strict feudal law which regulated the descent of a barony; certainly Stephen and probably Henry I had been chosen by the magnates in direct opposition to the declared wish of the last King. Now Henry wanted to establish the principle of hereditary succession, which was already more or less established in the Kingdom of France.

He may also have wished for a viceroy, with all the prestige of Coronation, to govern England as his deputy while he passed his life in his more civilized French dominions. Otherwise it is hard to see why he was in such a hurry. In 1170 he was only thirty-seven, and young Henry, his designated heir, just fifteen; as a matter of fact Henry II lived for nineteen years more and then died comparatively young, even for the short-lived middle ages. He was obviously very near making a permanent peace with his Archbishop, and if he had waited another year young Henry could have been crowned by Thomas, or his successor as Archbishop of Canterbury, in a perfectly regular fashion.

But Henry would not wait. His eldest son was old enough to bear arms, and of full age according to one interpretation of the feudal code (though if he had been a ward of the Crown as heir to a barony he would not have been his own master until he was twenty-one). In March King Henry crossed to England to begin the complicated negotiation which would lead to the crowning.

The negotiation was complicated because the consent of so many different people was required. The ceremony itself was new to England, though there were precedents in France, and many precedents in the Holy Roman Empire; the Emperor was in theory chosen by the free election of the magnates of Germany, but dynasties had arisen because Emperors had their eldest sons elected and crowned as soon as they came of age. In England it had been attempted once before, in the case of Stephen's son Eustace, but unsuccessfully; that made it more difficult than if it had never been tried at all. Every tenant-in-chief of the Crown had to be persuaded or bullied into swearing fealty to the heir, which he was not bound to do by the letter of the law. The King of France must be persuaded to give his consent to the inheritance of Normandy and Aquitaine. The Archbishop of Canterbury must consent to perform the rite, and the other Bishops to sanction it by their presence. It would give the ceremony more force if the Pope approved in advance, though perhaps that was not absolutely necessary. The King threw himself with great energy into the business of persuading all these people.

No one had any very strong objections. Young Henry was a gallant knight and very popular with all who knew him; he is nearly forgotten now, because he died without ruling, but his contemporaries esteemed him more highly than even his brother the Lionheart. Some Anglo-Norman magnates hesitated to throw away the opportunity of a brisk civil war when the throne should be vacant; but oversea there was plenty of fighting for those who enjoyed it, and it was on the whole better to have peace on your own estates while you jousted against the infidel in Outremer. The King of France was delighted to strengthen the principle that a crown descended by right to the eldest son of the last King; young Philip would find it useful when he himself came to die. The Bishops were in favour of any device that would keep the peace. The Pope and the Archbishop of Canterbury both approved the plan, though both sent reminders that only the Archbishop could crown a King of England. But terms of settlement had been arranged at the abortive conference on the hill of Montmartre; Henry had only to give the Kiss of Peace and Thomas would return to England and take up his duties. Nevertheless the Pope feared that Thomas might lose his temper when he met his suffragans, who had stayed quietly at home while he endured more than five years of penniless exile for the rights of the Church; that everything should pass off peacefully Alexander forbade the Archbishop to publish any sentences of excommunication until further orders.

King Henry still refused the Kiss; which seems to me strong evidence that in the spring of 1170 the death of the Archbishop had been already decided. Thomas was willing to come home for the Coronation, but would not start until he had received the Kiss. The King continued his preparations for the ceremony and the solemn banquet which came after, and began to argue that any Bishop could lawfully perform the rite, since past Kings of England had been validly crowned by the holders of other Sees. There were precedents in his favour, as precedents could be produced for almost any course of conduct in the historically-minded twelfth century. The Conqueror had been crowned by the Archbishop of York, not of Canterbury, for Stigand's elevation to Canterbury had been confirmed by an Antipope and was held to be uncanonical and void; and of course by going back far enough in time the royal clerks could find records of some very informal Saxon coronations. But that had nothing to do with the case. The Pope could make new Canon Law by his personal decree (though no secular potentate might alter the law of his land, even with the consent of his vassals), and if the Pope solemnly laid down that nowadays only the Archbishop of Canterbury might crown the King of England, then precedents were merely of historical interest.

Thomas wrote angrily to the Pope, saying that his quarrel with the King was by no means settled. He was convinced that Henry wanted only a temporary truce for the Coronation; and that as soon as the Young King was crowned the persecution of the Church would break out afresh. He begged to be granted his Legatine powers once more, so that the Bishops would be restrained by fear of excommunication from defying his orders. Alexander, obviously thinking that Thomas was complaining before he had been hurt, refused the Legatine powers; but he promised that he himself, with all the authority of the Holy See, would excommunicate any Bishop who defied his canonical superior.

In England it was commonly believed that the Pope had abandoned his headstrong supporter. If peace was about to be concluded on the King's terms the protests of a cantankerous exile might be disregarded. Roger of York in particular was pleased to score a point in the long controversy with the rival Archbishopric which endured to trouble Cardinal Wolsey more than three centuries later. He would prove to the world that he also was Archbishop and Metropolitan, with just as much power as that ridiculous Bailhache. Other Bishops took it for granted that the Pope would not upset the long-sought settlement over a mere punctilio, a brand-new privilege of Canterbury which in the nature of things could only be exercised at very rare intervals. Alexander would make a formal protest, of course, rather than desert a supporter who had suffered much for his obstinate loyalty; but he would not really be in earnest, and no serious punishment would follow.

On the 14th of June 1170 the Archbishop of York placed the crown on the head of the Young King in Westminster Abbey. The Bishops of London, Salisbury and Rochester were certainly present, and there may have been others; though we know that Winchester, Norwich and Exeter disapproved, and pointedly stayed away. But all the magnates did homage, and from this moment until his early death young Henry was undisputed King of England.

The game of twisting the Pope's tail to see how much he will stand was popular in twelfth-century England, as it still is in Catholic countries. But it is a dangerous amusement, especially for those who live too far from Rome to be in touch with the feeling of the Curia; for the public utterances of the Holy See are so stereotyped and bound by precedent that it is very hard to make out whether a protest is a conventional gesture of disapproval or an outburst of real anger. The English Bishops may well have felt surprise when Alexander brought out his thunderbolts; they had been given fair warning, but then they had heard so many other warnings.

It was the Bishops especially who felt his displeasure. No one blamed King Henry for taking what his clerks were willing to grant; he might reasonably persuade the Archbishop of York, though Archbishop Roger was wrong to allow himself to be persuaded. Even now the Pope did not broadcast his excommunications. He saw that the trouble in England was that the Church had been too long without a head, and he relied on Archbishop Thomas to reduce it to a proper state of discipline. He ordered his clerks to draw up sentences of excommunication against the Bishops of London and Salisbury, who had defied their Metropolitan, and of suspension only against Roger of York, who was under no duty to obey Canterbury and had merely usurped the privilege of a rival. But when these documents had been sealed with the great seal of almighty Rome he sent them to Thomas, telling him to use his own discretion whether to publish them or not. Perhaps the defiant Bishops would apologize and promise future obedience when they learned what weapons he had in his desk; in any case, this procedure avoided the danger of giving full Legatine power to Thomas himself, which he might have used to excommunicate the whole population of England.

King Henry, who had visited London for the Coronation, where he had emphasized his son's new status by serving him with his own hands at the solemn banquet, returned almost at once to his French dominions. He was urgently needed, for the Young King's wife, the princess whom Thomas had escorted from Paris twelve years ago, had not been crowned with her husband; and her father talked of avenging the slighted honour of his family by the traditional method of ravaging the Vexin. But Henry had just got his way in a difficult and important matter, and he was in one of his very rare moods of good temper. He found a simple solution to the problem of etiquette. Let the Young King be crowned all over again, with his wife; that would make his title all the stronger, and they could hold another really good banquet in Westminster Hall. Best of all, this time the Archbishop of Canterbury could perform the ceremony, and everybody would be satisfied.

The exiled clerks had begun to negotiate for themselves, hoping to get some of the income of their English benefices. But when envoys met the hasty and bad-mannered King direct negotiations were always at the mercy of impromptu exchanges of abuse. Herbert of Bosham, the gallant chaplain who had arranged the escape from Northampton, obtained a public audience with King Henry, but the King greeted him with the wounding phrase, 'Here comes the priest's son'.

That was literally true, though misleading. After the death of his wife Herbert's father had taken priest's orders as a widower. But of course Henry implied that Herbert was the bastard of a celibate priest. Herbert indignantly pointed out the facts of the case, and followed with a devastating answer. 'It is wrong to call me a priest's son,' he said, 'for my father was not a priest when I was born. Just as it would be wrong to call a man the son of a King, unless his father had been King when he was born.'

Everyone gasped, for this general remark had a very personal application. King Henry's ancestors in the male line had never been more than Counts of Anjou, and his hereditary claim to the crown of England came only through the father of his mother; in medieval eyes he was not of royal birth. It was the sort of thing that only a companion of the Archbishop would dare to say in the King's presence, and as Henry brought the interview to an end in an explosion of wrath one baron muttered, 'I don't care whose son he is, the brave man. I only wish I had a son like him.' Even the King's party respected the courage of Thomas and his followers.

But exchanges of this kind brought agreement no nearer, and the sudden reconciliation which followed is the most puzzling incident in Thomas's otherwise straightforward life. On the 22nd of July at Freteval in Normandy he rode up to King Henry and dismounted to kneel before him. The King immediately dismounted and embraced him, and then held the stirrup for him to mount; but the onlookers noted that the embrace did not include the formal Kiss which meant peace. Within a very short time it had been agreed that the endowments of Canterbury should be restored and the exiles forgiven; that was

easily done, for the terms had been arranged at Montmartre. Then the King and the Archbishop rode off side
by side, chatting excitedly, and seeming to pick up the
threads of the old intimacy which had been severed so
abruptly seven years ago. Nothing had been said about
the Constitutions of Clarendon, or appeals to Rome, or
any of the other matters in dispute. If Thomas was content with a mere promise of friendship and just dealing,
not even ratified by the Kiss, he might have had exactly
those terms any time during the last six years. Why was
he so easily satisfied?

There are three possible explanations. The courtiers
noted that King Henry was in an unusually sunny mood,
and Thomas may have mistaken it for a genuine change
of heart; if the King honestly desired the good government of the Church in England then the Constitutions
might not be an insurmountable obstacle to friendly
relations, any more than very similar customs had prevented co-operation between the Conqueror and Archbishop Lanfranc. Or Thomas may have given way to
the Pope's strong desire for peace with the King of
England, and decided that it was more important for
Alexander to keep a valuable ally in his struggle with the
Emperor than for the English Church to enjoy unfettered
intercourse with Rome. Or, the most likely reason in my
opinion, he may have understood that a genuine peace
was impossible, since the King would not keep the
promises of friendship and fair dealing which he scattered
so lavishly; but he may also have seen that the exchange
of letters across the breadth of Christendom would never
settle anything, and that the only way to restore discipline
among the Bishops was for him to return to Canterbury

at the risk of death; a risk which never daunted the warrior who had stormed the walls of Cahors.

Although he had consented to return he still delayed his journey, hoping to receive that elusive Kiss of Peace. Meanwhile he began to put his affairs in order, and to seek reports on the administration of the lands of Canterbury during his exile. He learned that Ranulf de Broc had conducted himself as a tyrant, especially to the monks of Christ Church, and he therefore excommunicated him as a despoiler of church property; he might do that without reference to the Pope, merely in the exercise of his episcopal power, for Broc lived in his own diocese of Canterbury. Then he heard that the second Coronation would not take place until the spring of 1171, and that it was hoped King Henry would keep Christmas in England. He decided to return with the King, so that they might make a fresh start together.

There was still the question of the Kiss of Peace. Since Henry attached such importance to this superstitious performance he would presumably consider himself bound by it even if it was extorted by a trick. Thomas made a rather pathetic attempt to trick his sovereign into honourable behaviour. On the 12th of October he suddenly entered the King's chapel at Amboise just as Mass was about to begin. In those days, at the point in the Mass when the celebrant says 'The Peace of the Lord be with you always', it was the custom that he should bestow a kiss on the most important member of the congregation; he would kiss the man next to him in rank, and so the kiss would travel through the church, until all who heard the same Mass were united in concord. When everyone was aware of his social precedence in any company this charming little ceremony caused no trouble. But in later times there were scandalous struggles for precedence at the altar-rail, and the Kiss is no longer given to laymen; though you may still see it travelling down the ranks of the canons and deacons at Capitular High Mass in Westminster Cathedral.

Of course the King of England would receive the first Kiss; but the Archbishop of Canterbury was next in rank to the King, and Henry would be compelled by the strong bonds of medieval etiquette to pass it directly to him. This he was determined never to do, and he very nearly refused to hear his morning Mass; which would have been as uncouth and extraordinary at that period as if nowadays a King should not bother to shave every day. The royal chaplain was aware of the dilemma, and he unexpectedly began a Mass of Requiem for a departed soul in Purgatory, in which the words of peace are not said and the Kiss is not given; though the 12th of October is the feast of St. Wilfred of York, and it was very surprising that the King of England should ignore one of the most famous English saints.

When Mass was finished Thomas approached the King, and directly begged him to grant the Kiss before they left the chapel. Henry answered that this was not a suitable occasion, though he might grant it later on, at some festival when there were plenty of great men present to bear witness to the reconciliation. Thomas realized, at last, that the settlement had only been made to be broken, and that Henry was still his foe. He left Amboise immediately, and prepared to cross to England without waiting for the King.

CHAPTER TWELVE

THE RETURN

It was important, for the peace of England and the strengthening of the title of the Young King, that Henry should give the impression in public that he was on good terms with his Archbishop. When Thomas reached Rouen with his clerks and baggage-train he found the King had sent an imposing escort to do him honour on the journey. But the official in charge was John of Oxford, who was said to have sworn obedience to the Antipope at Wurzburg, and whose elevation to be Dean of Salisbury while excommunicate had brought about the excommunication of that unfortunate seeker after an impossible neutrality, Bishop Jocelyn of Salisbury. He was still a royal official, and perhaps he specialized in arranging journeys of state; but his appointment to wait on the Archbishop at this juncture could be nothing but a calculated insult.

On the 24th of November 1170 Thomas reached Witsand, the haven in Normandy which led to the easiest crossing to England (Boulogne and Calais owed allegiance to the Court of Flanders; they would not normally be used by loyal subjects of the King of England). There he halted for a week, to learn the latest news from his Province and to make up his mind what to do with the Papal sentences which he still carried unpublished in his baggage. What he heard was very shocking, and decided him to impose the penalties which were the immediate cause of his murder.

In the first place, at Michaelmas, the 29th of September, the profits of the lands of Canterbury had been paid to the King's officials; that was the day, with the harvest safely gathered, when agricultural rents were paid, and there would be no more profit from those estates until Michaelmas 1171. But as far back as the 22nd of July, when the crops were still ripening in the fields, the King had promised to restore the endowments of Canterbury. Thomas would remain penniless for another year, and Henry had already broken the terms of his agreement.

That might be regarded as merely another example of the financial sharp practice for which Henry was always notorious. In any case a Bishop looks a little ridiculous if he invokes spiritual penalties to recover money owing to him, though that is no reason why he should be cheated. What was much worse was the continual open insubordination of those very Bishops who had already put themselves in the wrong by sanctioning or taking part in the irregular Coronation.

During the exile there had been no elections to Bishoprics, for it was customary for the Metropolitan to consecrate a new suffragan (though in strict Canon Law any Bishop can consecrate another Bishop). But several Bishops had died in the last six years, and the Sees of Lincoln, Hereford, Chichester, Ely and Bath were vacant. The normal procedure would be for the clergy of the Cathedral chapter to assemble, in the presence of the Archbishop and the other Bishops of the Province; then a letter from the King would be read, giving his leave to elect, probably with a pretty direct indication of the individual on whom he thought their choice should fall; and if the Archbishop and his suffragans raised no objection the King's will would be carried into effect. But Henry evidently supposed that Thomas, still not reconciled by the Kiss of Peace, would veto every royal nomination. He was determined to seize this last chance of filling the bench of Bishops with subservient royal clerks, and since the Primate was no longer technically in exile a bold lawyer might hold that these elections took place with his approval. The King had therefore summoned a chosen delegation of clergy from the vacant Cathedrals to elect in his presence, where they would not dare to disappoint his wishes; the Archbishop of York, and the Bishops of London and Salisbury, were actually on the English coast, waiting for a favourable wind to cross the Channel and consecrate the King's nominees in Normandy.

If Thomas was not to be harassed for years by five young Bishops of the King's party there was not a moment to lose. On the 31st of November he published the Papal excommunications of London and Salisbury, and the Papal suspension of Roger of York, who was always treated more leniently since he owed no obedience to Canterbury. He then embarked, and actually passed the ship bearing the rebellious Bishops, who crossed to Normandy on the same day.

On the 1st of December he landed at his own town of Sandwich, for he feared arrest if he entered the King's port of Dover. The reconciliation of Freteval was now a dead letter, and the end of his exile only meant that the struggle was transferred from France to England. All

Kent was in a turmoil. The sheriff had mustered the militia, lest the vassals of Canterbury should rally in arms to defend their lord; Dover was strongly garrisoned, and the castellan had decided to send Thomas straight back to Normandy if he could catch him; Ranulf de Broc had gathered his numerous and turbulent kin in Saltwood Castle, swearing he would hold it by force if the King commanded him to restore it to its rightful lord; the clergy and burgesses of Canterbury were ringing the bells and decorating the streets to celebrate the return of the Confessor who had made the name of his See famous in all Christendom; the peasants thronged the high roads, kneeling for the blessing of the holy man who was their traditional protector against royal oppression. Thomas rode straight to Canterbury, but at the town gate he dismounted and walked through the streets; from his throne, the throne of St. Augustine which still remains in the Cathedral, he joined in the hymns of rejoicing which were sung for many hours by a packed congregation. Then he returned to his palace, part of the monastery of Christ Church, and began to take up the reins of his long-neglected administration.

For a week he remained quietly in Canterbury, partly to give time for popular excitement to die down, partly because there was much pressing business to be done. He absolved those monks who had been illegally intruded during his exile, thus regularizing their position and demonstrating that he would not stand on the letter of his rights if no principle was involved. There were ordinations and confirmations to be held, and a multitude of lay vassals who had inherited fiefs of the Honour of Canterbury, and newly-installed rectors of benefices in the diocese, who must personally tender their feudal oaths or their clerical promises of obedience.

The rebellious Bishops landed at Witsand while Thomas was landing at Sandwich. They were appalled to discover they had incurred a Papal ban; though they had come prepared to appeal against an excommunication pronounced merely by the Archbishop of Canterbury. The proposed election of new Bishops was abandoned without question; the excommunicates rode to the King's court, and begged Henry to use all his influence at Rome to get them absolved as quickly as possible; they also sent messengers to England, expressing sincere repentance and begging Thomas to absolve them. He answered that he would absolve his subjects, London and Salisbury, if they came before him in person and made suitable apology; but that he had no power to remove the suspension of Roger of York, who was his equal and not his suffragan. In normal times any Archbishop of York would have been delighted to get such an admission from his rival of Canterbury; but Roger now saw himself faced with an uncomfortable and expensive journey over the Alps, and his bitter complaint to the King was the chief cause of Henry's fatal loss of temper.

After an inoffensive week of diocesan affairs Thomas considered it was time to approach the actual ruler of England, the fifteen-year-old Young King. Little Henry had learned courtesy as a page in the Chancellor's household, and in the middle ages that was considered a very strong sentimental bond. Though Thomas had tried to stop the Coronation he had never opposed the scheme by which the Kingdom should devolve on the King's eldest surviving son. In fact he had never had occasion to quarrel with the young man, and he hoped to make a fresh start with a new government.

The Young King was then at Winchester, but an Angevin court was extremely mobile; he had arranged to keep Christmas at Woodstock, and it was rumoured that he might visit Westminster on the way. Thomas decided to visit London, where it was customary for the Legate of the whole English Church to spend a good deal of his time; he hoped to meet young Henry without lowering his dignity by making a special journey to court as though he were suing for pardon and mercy. But first he prepared the ground with care. He chose a really valuable Christmas present, such as would delight the heart of any boy who had just received the honour of knighthood; and he sent an important member of his family, the Prior of St. Martin's at Dover, who became the next Archbishop of Canterbury, to deliver it in person.

The present was three fine war-horses. Thomas was an excellent horseman, experienced in stable management, and war-horses chosen by him would be worthy to carry a King; in the twelfth century there was an enormous difference in value between the hack that even a gentleman rode on a journey and a war-horse trained to obey the bridle-arm of a rider hampered with a heavy shield; a few years later William the Marshal was compelled to leave old King Henry's court in a hurry and for 16s. he bought a hack for the journey; then the Count of Flanders gave him a generous present, and after prolonged bargaining he bought for £60 a war-horse for which he later refused £100.

Having despatched his gift Thomas set out for London; Rochester welcomed him with crowds in the decorated streets and services of thanksgiving in the Cathedral; as he neared Southwark the guilds of London marched in procession over their bridge to greet the city's most famous native son, and bells rang in all the close-packed steeples. But on the bridge he was met by a royal messenger, who told him that the Young King would not accept gifts from his father's foe, and that in these disturbed times the Archbishop of Canterbury should dwell quietly in his See. Since Thomas passed a night in his suburban manor of Harrow he must have crossed the Thames, but perhaps he was ferried over outside the city walls; certainly the official welcome of the burgesses of London was cancelled at the last minute. On the 13th of December he rode back to Canterbury, a declared enemy of the ruler of England, hardly to be protected by the King's Peace; while throughout the land the inspired lunatics, talking animals, and miraculous images which expressed the popular feeling of the twelfth century continually uttered prophecies of doom.

In Canterbury he was in some danger from the turbulent Ranulf de Broc, who still held Saltwood Castle and was beginning to wage private war on the Archbishop's servants. A ship laden with the heavy baggage he had collected in exile was driven out of its course and beached near Saltwood. Ranulf pillaged the cargo, his brother Robert ambushed the train of pack-horses which bore the remnants towards Canterbury, and his nephew John expressed his contempt by cutting off the tail of a horse intended for the Archbishop's own riding. This was a peculiarly deadly insult, and Thomas replied by excommunicating all the Brocs; Ranulf received the news of his punishment with the ominous boast that a man under excommunication could fall no further, and that he had heard how such sinners were expected to behave.

(This cutting off of the horse's tail is worth a note. In the middle ages it was believed that all natives of England were afflicted with tails. One of the companions of St. Augustine, insulted by heathen Saxons somewhere in Dorset, cursed his attackers and their children to wear tails for ever after. But in time the curse wore off, to be revived, for Kent only, in revenge for this insult to the Archbishop of Canterbury. That every man born in Kent has a tail, of which he is heartily ashamed, is an opinion still frequently expressed in Sussex. If any of my readers was born in Kent, without a tail, he may congratulate himself that even this renewal of the curse is beginning to weaken.)

On the 19th of December Thomas held an ordination in his Cathedral, and on the 21st he celebrated his fifty-second and last birthday with a solemn High Mass in honour of St. Thomas the Apostle. He must have known that death was near, but he continued his duties as though he would live for ever.

CHAPTER THIRTEEN

THE MURDER

On Christmas Day there are three different Masses, and Thomas celebrated at least two of them at the High Altar of his Cathedral. He also preached to the great throng of laymen who crowded the nave to welcome their feudal lord and spiritual father. But his sermon was very ominous. He took as his text the correct rendering of a passage wrongly translated in the Authorized Version: 'Peace on earth to men of goodwill.' That is not a promise of universal concord; on the contrary, it implies a threat of divine anger against those who lack goodwill towards God, and Thomas knew that the King wished evil to the Church. He reminded the congregation that they stood in a specially hallowed building; many holy Archbishops lay buried there, and one in particular, St. Alphege, done to death by a drunken gang of heathen Danes, was a canonized martyr; it seemed very likely that they would soon possess the bones of another martyred Archbishop. Like the hero of a Norse Saga, he was aware of his approaching death as soon as it was planned. It had already been planned.

The usual story is that Roger of York complained to the King at his Christmas feast that Thomas would not withdraw his suspension. That hardly leaves time for a journey from Normandy to Kent, and probably the deciding outburst of Henry's unbalanced rage was actually uttered a few days earlier. It was certainly the suspension of the Archbishop of York which was the immediate cause. We do not know exactly what the King said; he spoke in French, and the historians wrote in Latin; but one early version runs like this: 'What sluggards, what cowards, have I brought up in my court, who care nothing for their allegiance to their lord! Not one will deliver me from this low-born priest!'

That was a direct incitement to murder. Afterwards Henry's only excuse was that he so habitually uttered insane threats that sensible courtiers disregarded anything he said in his childish tantrums. Like a silly little boy who threatens to run away from home because he cannot get his own way in everything, Henry only wanted some calm grown-up person to make a fuss of him and coax him into a better humour. But four of his household knights, Reginald fitzUrse, William de Tracy, Richard le Breton, and Hugh de Morville, decided to go to Canterbury at once; they would compel the Archbishop to give way, or bring him back a prisoner. Probably when they left the King's court they did not intend to cut down an unarmed priest, but they were determined to use more and more force until they achieved their object. It was afterwards believed that before they set out they had a private interview with Roger of York, and that he approved their plan; but this may be malicious gossip.

They crossed the Channel separately, fearing to alarm the Archbishop's adherents in Kent, and met again at Saltwood Castle, where of course Ranulf de Broc welcomed them and promised them the assistance of his strong garrison. When they rode to Canterbury on the 29th of December they were at the head of a considerable band, including the numerous and bloodthirsty family of Broc.

On that afternoon Thomas had finished dinner, but he was still chatting at his private table with a few monks and clerks, while the servants who had waited on him and the rest of the Archbishop's household dined at a long table in the body of the hall. Some historians have made an unnecessary difficulty about the time of day, since we are told it was the ninth hour (after sunrise) and yet it seems to grow dark immediately afterwards; they forget that in the twelfth century each day, and each night, were divided into twelve hours, and that therefore at midwinter the hours of daylight did not contain anything like sixty modern minutes. The doors of the hall stood open, for soon the poor of Canterbury would be admitted to carry off any food that remained, and the four knights entered without challenge; they were unarmed, and attracted no particular attention. They walked up the long room to the Archbishop's table, and since there were no vacant seats they squatted among the rushes on the floor. There was nothing odd in that; in a medieval hall there were few benches and hardly any chairs, and a great many people habitually sat on the floor, or heaped the rushes into a bundle so that they could reach the food on the table.

Thomas recognized the newcomers as household knights of the King; but they did not present a letter, and he probably thought it rude of them to stroll in uninvited; for some minutes he continued his conversation, and then casually asked them their business. They began to clamour that he should absolve the Bishops, and he refused; there were angry words on both sides, until presently the knights rushed out to the courtyard. On their way they encountered the steward of the estates of Canterbury, a layman named William fitzNigel. He must have been a very great coward, for he at once rushed up to Thomas and withdrew his allegiance, explaining that he dared not face the King's anger. Thomas dismissed him from his service, and he went outside to join the following of the knights; presumably he hoped his local knowledge would make him a valued and highly-rewarded accomplice, but the Brocs knew every stone of the building and did not need him. He does not appear again in this story, and his name is only recorded because he was the only coward to be found in Canterbury that evening.

The courtyard was within the enclosure of the Abbey, where normally decorum reigned. Now it was full of angry warriors, and the four knights could be seen donning their mail, servants hovering round to fasten the straps (no knight could arm himself without assistance). The monks took alarm, fearing a plot to kidnap the Archbishop; they barred the door of the hall and begged Thomas to take sanctuary in the Cathedral.

Thomas had made up his mind from the first that he would be killed before he would surrender. He was not afraid of death, but his training in Canon Law reminded him that if murder was committed in the Cathedral it would automatically be desecrate, and no services might be held in it until it had been reconsecrated. He may also have feared that if the rioters were thwarted they would commence a general massacre of the inhabitants of Christ Church; in fact his whole attitude that evening showed a desire to get the killing over quickly, without involving others. He refused to leave the hall.

The monks thought the knights were probably drunk and certainly blind with rage; their chief idea seems to have been to put obstacles in their path, without actually offering armed resistance, until someone in authority arrived to quell the disturbance. The servants had already fled through an inner door which opened on the cloister between the hall and the Cathedral; a few monks followed them, and the rest once more begged the Archbishop to escape. Thomas answered that monks were notoriously timid, and that there was nothing to fear. 'It is not fitting', he added, 'that a church should be polluted with the blood of a sinner. Whatever comes must be borne with patience.'

It was now time for Vespers, and the daily office is the chief reason for the existence of a monastery; the routine of prayer must continue in the midst of any calamity. The monks had a decent excuse for leaving, and most of them walked through the cloister to their accustomed places in choir. At the same time the knights and their followers, baulked by the great iron-bound door of the hall, began to explore the courtyard. A carpenter who had been repairing an outside staircase fled in panic, leaving his tools; Reginal fitzUrse picked up a hatchet, and Robert de Broc found an unbarred door leading into the other end of the range of stone buildings of which the hall formed part. The partitions between the rooms were only plaster on a frame of wickerwork; a few strokes of the hatchet hewed them down, and Robert de Broc entered the hall to unbar the main door from the inside.

Thomas now feared that the mob might lynch all his companions; if he was to offer his life in seemly fashion he must get away by himself. He announced that he would join the monks at Vespers, and hastened through the inner door into the cloister. His clerks followed, and the hall was left empty.

But the customary passage from the hall to the Cathedral was thronged with armed men. The anxious little party had to go round the other side of the cloister, which was seldom used. Suddenly they were confronted with a bolted door; a clerk charged it with his shoulder, and as the bolt fell to the ground it flew open; which may have been a miracle, but probably proves only that the Brocs had neglected the fabric and the bolt was rusted through. Looking back, the fugitives could see the hall they had just left filling with rioters, who milled about trying to summon the courage necessary to invade the sanctuary of the Cathedral.

Thomas was being very difficult. Obviously his aim was to remain alone in the cloister while his companions reached the safety of the Cathedral. To begin with he said he would go no farther until his cross was borne before him, in the regular ritual for an Archbishop visiting his own Cathedral; his customary cross-bearer had been sent to France with letters, but a clerk named Henry of Auxerre fetched the cross and preceded him in due form. Then he insisted on walking last, the place of honour in an ecclesiastical procession; he loitered to watch the intruders, but his companions, careless of etiquette, caught hold of him and hustled him along.

Meanwhile Vespers had begun, but the singing was very ragged; for a rumour was going round the choir that the Archbishop had just been murdered in his own hall. Two lay servants, who lodged in an upper room of the cloister, had unlocked a seldom-used door of the Cathedral and burst in with this startling news. It was a remarkable chance that they used this door, for it was the one that Thomas and his companions reached a moment later. I think myself that Thomas had counted on finding it locked, in accordance with his plan to meet death on unconsecrated ground; but seeing it so strangely open he permitted himself to be pushed through it, though he delayed until all his companions were safely inside.

William fitzStephen (a clerk who afterwards wrote the best biography of the martyr) stepped forward to welcome his Archbishop. 'Stay with us, father,' he said, 'that if need be we may suffer together and together be glorified. We have been distracted by your absence; now let us be consoled by your presence.' A very proper, rather bogus, speech; as he presently ran away it represents rather what he thought he ought to have felt than his actual sentiments.

The fugitives looked back, and saw the cloister filling with their pursuers. The knights came first, wearing full mail with the new-fashioned great helms which covered the whole face; they could be identified only by the devices on their shields. They waved their swords, shouting 'King's men!', the war-cry of the royal household. But their followers, grooms, servants, and the garrison of Saltwood Castle, remained nervously in the background, fearing to enter the Cathedral.

Vespers had been broken off unfinished. Apart from the candles in the choir the Cathedral must have been pitch-dark, and the cloister very shadowy. Some monks began to disperse into the gloom of the side-chapels and triforium, the inner arcade which forms a gallery round the choir high in the wall. But the bravest, and his own family of clerks, clustered round Thomas. Someone began to bolt the doors, but the Archbishop forbade it. 'I command you, by your oath of obedience, to leave the doors open,' he said. 'A church should not be made a castle.'

He might have hidden successfully. All the monks of Christ Church were scattered through the dark Cathedral, and not one was found. If he had remained in hiding until dawn he could have been smuggled away; and the Young King would send to restore order as soon as he heard of the riot. But Thomas, who had stormed Cahors and unhorsed Engelram de Trie before the assembled armies of France and Normandy, began to feel the rage of battle. Hitherto he had accepted patiently the martyrdom which was to be his fate, lingering in the cloister that death might come swiftly; now he determined to meet his foes face to face, possibly hoping to abash them by his pride and courage, possibly surrendering to an overmastering desire to say what he thought of them before they struck. A monk named Grim of Cambridge, the only Saxon present, picked up his cross, for Henry of Auxerre had fled; Thomas now turned to him in fierce exultation. 'In the Lord's battle I shall fight it out toe to toe,' he shouted. It was a war-cry.

But his sense of theatrical effect did not desert him; if an Archbishop was to be slain in his own Cathedral the throne by the High Altar was obviously the correct setting for the tragedy. He walked eastward, and had just begun to ascend a short flight of steps leading from the north transept to the choir when the knights rushed in from the cloister. By this time all his companions had fled, save three: Canon William fitzStephen, who had welcomed him, Prior Robert of Merton his confessor and school-fellow, and Grim the Saxon, who clung staunchly to the cross he had volunteered to carry as though it were a standard in the press of a hard-fought battle.

The knights shouted war-cries and waved their swords, for only if they kept up the surge of excitement which had carried them from the hall to the Cathedral could they bring themselves to lay hands on an Archbishop. Their plan was perhaps to bind him and lead him prisoner before the King, not to murder him. Inside the door they checked, unable to discern anything in the December darkness of the great church. FitzUrse took the lead, advancing into the blackness with a sword in one hand and the carpenter's hatchet in the other. 'Where is the traitor,' he shouted, 'where is Thomas Becket?'

It was a calculated insult to call Thomas of London, Archbishop of Canterbury, by the middle-class nickname of his father. Thomas halted, looking back to the figures outlined against the last of the dusk; but he did not answer. Then fitzUrse saw something move in the gloom, and shouted again, 'Where is the Archbishop?'

That was the very last chance. Thomas must flee instantly, or meet the challenge. He walked down the steps, determined to confront his assailants, and answered hotly: 'Here I am, no traitor, but priest and Archbishop.'

FitzUrse made his final offer. 'Absolve the King's Bishops,' he called, and Thomas, still approaching, curtly answered 'No'.

At the foot of the steps was a little side-altar dedicated to Our Lady, its reredos shutting it off from the nave; to the east a party wall ran out to the lowest of the steps leading to the choir; in this little corner, isolated from the main body of the enormous church, Thomas took his stand for his last battle. He recognized fitzUrse, either by his voice or from the bear blazoned on his shield (for each knight's face was hidden by his helm), and recalled that this was one of his own vassals, holding land of the Honour of Canterbury. It is characteristic of Thomas the knight and warrior that what outraged his sense of the fitness of things was not that the King's knights should attack an Archbishop, but that a vassal should lift his hand against his lord. 'What dost thou want with me?' he asked, employing the contemptuous French second person singular, used normally to servants and inferiors. 'Your death,' fitzUrse replied; and I think, though this is my personal opinion, that this was the first time any knight had purposed to kill Thomas there and then. They had hoped to truss him up and bring him a prisoner to Normandy, and in fact they made one more effort to capture him.

Thomas had his answer ready. He must have been composing it in his mind ever since he left the hall, for it was a considerable speech, expressed in regular rhetorical form; but he was a trained lawyer and scholar, used to thinking on his feet and speaking correctly.

'I accept death', he said, 'in the name of the Lord, and I commend my soul and the cause of the Church to God and Blessed Mary and the patron saints of Canterbury. But by the authority which God has given me I interdict you from harming any of my followers.'

As the knights closed in Grim still held the cross beside his leader. William fitzStephen and Robert of Merton play no further part in the story, and presumably they fled about this time. But there were many witnesses of what followed, for a crowd of Canterbury burgesses had gathered in the great west door; they were trying to summon the resolution to rescue their lord in spite of the mailed knights; if the attackers delayed for further parley their victim might yet escape.

FitzUrse threw down his hatchet (it lay on the floor all night, and was afterwards preserved in the Cathedral, one of the principal relics of the martyrdom); he struck with his sword, and the blow knocked the cap from Thomas's head, but Thomas remained unharmed. On the face of it this is a puzzling episode; a trained swordsman could hardly miss a stationary target so completely. It has been interpreted as a blow of blind and uncalculated fury. I think it was an extremely skilful stroke, which exactly accomplished its object. When a knight was captured in the field the victor symbolically grasped his helm, and if he had no time to lead his prisoner to the rear he merely removed it; a bareheaded man dared not escape among the swords of the mêlée. Thus fitzUrse formally struck off the cap to make the Archbishop his prisoner. The next action of the attackers confirms this interpretation, for they surged round Thomas trying to lift him up bodily and put him on the shoulders of William de Tracy, who stood ready to carry him out of the Cathedral.

Thomas was resigned to martyrdom, but he could not endure that his own vassal should send a sword whistling past his ears. He shouted at fitzUrse: 'Reginald, you pander, *you* must not touch me. You owe me fealty and service!'

FitzUrse answered: 'I owe you no fealty, no service, against my fealty to the King my liege-lord.'

Grim jumped behind his leader and caught hold of him

round the waist; as the knights tried to drag him away the two clerks pulled back, struggling fiercely, doing all that unarmed men could do against mailed knights. Thomas, immensely tall, towered over the whole struggle. He seized fitzUrse by the skirts of his mail, and gave such a mighty tug that the recreant staggered, and nearly fell to the ground. The knights saw they would never take him alive; and they must finish the business quickly, for the crowd of burgesses was beginning to advance from the west door. Hugh de Morville ran off to keep them at bay, and so avoided the worst guilt of that awful night. The other three drew back, and then closed in, swords aloft, for the kill.

Thomas raised his hands in the attitude of prayer; but also to shut out sight of the swords. It is as difficult for a trained swordsman to take a blow on the head without parrying or dodging as it is for a trained boxer to take a punch on the chin without making some effort to duck. Thomas was a skilled warrior, and he was determined not to flinch. For that reason, not from any fear of death, he covered his eyes. But Grim was still full of fight. As fitzUrse struck the first blow he tried to parry it with his cross; the sword nearly severed his arm, and then wounded Thomas on the head, a glancing blow which cut off the top of his scalp, the sacred tonsure of a priest. Grim collapsed, having done far more than his duty; it was fitting that a Saxon should defend this Norman warrior who was dying for the whole English Church. But Thomas still stood erect, commending his soul to St. Denys of Paris and St. Alphege of Canterbury, both Archbishops and both martyrs.

Then William de Tracy struck and struck again, and

at the third blow Thomas went down; but he still struggled to raise himself on his hands, muttering, so low that only the gallant Grim overheard, 'For the name of Jesus and the safety of the Church I am ready to face death'.

Then he lay prostrate, but his last dying action was to arrange his gown decorously over his feet, that his body might lie decently in his Father's house until it was taken up for burial.

Richard le Breton had not struck a blow. But fitzUrse and Tracy were determined that he should share their guilt; there must be no relatively innocent accomplices to bear witness against them. Urged by his companions he aimed a mighty stroke at the fallen Archbishop, shouting: 'Take this for love of my lord William, the King's brother!' (Nearly ten years ago Thomas had hindered William's marriage with the rich heiress Isabel de Warenne; evidently the injury still rankled.) The sword struck the open wound on the scalp, and smashed the skull; then the point hit the stone pavement on which the martyr lay, and snapped from the blade. Richard dropped his broken sword, and it became another of the chief relics of the martyrdom, exposed on the special Altar of the Sword.

These frightened angry men hesitated over the body, unwilling to strike again yet not quite certain that Thomas was really dead. Remember that all this was done in almost total darkness, the only light a few candles in the choir. So dark was it that no one recognized Grim, a stranger from Cambridge; Tracy thought he was the eminent John of Salisbury, Thomas's old friend who often carried his cross, and boasted next day that they had cut down the famous Papalist writer. But there was in the

Cathedral a man even more bloodthirsty than these knights, who was determined to make sure. Hugh of Horsea was a clerk, already known by the nickname of the Evil Deacon; though we are not informed of the particular crime which had earned him this distinction; he had followed the knights from the hall to the Cathedral, because he hated his Archbishop and rejoiced to see harm done to him. This scoundrel now came forward and inserted the point of his sword into the gaping wound in the skull. He twisted his weapon, scattering the brains on the pavement, and then said cheerfully (I translate freely from the stilted contemporary Latin): 'Come on, boys, let's go. That chap won't get up again.'

The murderers crept out silently, and rode back to Saltwood. The body of the martyr lay alone before Our Lady's altar, until the bravest of the monks of Christ Church emerged from their hiding-places to prepare it for burial.

CHAPTER FOURTEEN

AFTER THE MURDER

The news of the crime sent a thrill of horror through all Christendom. The Pope, once more back in Rome, at once ordered a Requiem Mass in his Basilica of the Lateran, Mother and Head of All the Churches of the City and the World. But while the canons were singing 'Requiem in Aeternum', the prayer for a departed soul in Purgatory, an angel appeared in the roof and led them in the Introit 'Laetabitur Justus', which gives thanks that another martyr has been added to the Heavenly Host, and all the black vestments of mourning were miraculously changed to martyr's red. This anecdote does not rest on such good authority as the rest of my history, and no one need believe it unless he wishes; but it represents accurately the public opinion of the day.

King Henry was terrified lest all his vassals should throw off their allegiance. He swore in public that he had not instigated the murder, and then hastily went off to Ireland, that uncivilized region at the ends of the earth where no Papal messengers could reach him. In 1172 he ventured back to Normandy, and at Avranches was formally absolved by Papal Legates sent specially for the purpose. As I have already said, no medieval judge ever tried to bring home guilt to a suspect who swore he was innocent; but Henry may have been telling the truth as he saw it. Certainly he had incited to murder, but perhaps he did not expect anyone to take seriously his ill-tempered ravings.

Archbishop Roger of York insisted on taking a public oath of innocence. To begin with no one had suspected him, but after that it was universally taken for granted that he had encouraged the murderers.

Canterbury Cathedral was polluted with blood. For nearly a year it lay empty, the altars stripped and the holy images covered as though every day were Good Friday. On the feast of St. Thomas the Apostle, the 21st of December 1171, which would have been the martyr's fifty-third birthday, it was solemnly reconsecrated, and from that day until the Reformation the holiest spot in it was the tomb of St. Thomas the Martyr. But because the 29th of December is not a good season for pilgrimage in the climate of Kent, the chief festival was held on the 7th of July, the anniversary of the dedication of the magnificent shrine; that is the feast to which Chaucer's pilgrims rode, though the 2nd of December, the anniversary of Thomas's last return to England, was also kept in memory. In 1174 King Henry himself made pilgrimage to the shrine of his great adversary (who had been solemnly canonized in 1173); things were going very badly for him at that time, but while he was being scourged in penance by the monks of Christ Church, the King of Scotland, his most dangerous foe, was captured in a thick fog outside the walls of besieged Alnwick; he was greatly encouraged by this coincidence, for it seemed to show that his old comrade in arms was helping him from his throne in Heaven, as he had helped him before Toulouse.

All Henry's children hated their father, and indeed no

one who knew him intimately liked him; in Thomas he had murdered his solitary friend. His three daughters married William the Good King of Sicily, Alfonso III King of Castile, and William the Lion Duke of Saxony. To vex their father they spread the martyr's cult in their new homes, and within a few years he was venerated from Acre in Outremer to remote Iceland. His fellow-townsmen of London held him in especial honour; his image guarded their bridge and figured on the common seal of their Corporation; he was patron of the London brewers, who remembered his efforts to advertise English ale in France, and of the vintners of Venice, who admired him as a connoisseur of good wine. Churches all over England were dedicated to him, though of course at the Reformation they were rededicated to St. Thomas the Apostle; for King Henry VIII had a particular dislike of an Archbishop who had defied a King. The Church of Rome still venerates him as a great saint, patron and protector of the Venerable English College in Rome and of the secular clergy of England; and in England his feast is a double of the first class.

Thrilling stories were told of the awful fate which pursued the murderers; but the actual truth is rather prosaic. As soon as they understood that Henry would not reward them for their crime they fled to Scotland. The King of Scotland took pride in sheltering fugitives from English justice, because it emphasized his rather precarious independence; at first he promised to protect them, but presently he was forced to withdraw his pledge, because all his own subjects kept on trying to hang them from the nearest tree. They returned to England and shut themselves in the strong castle of Knaresborough (Yorks) while they negotiated terms of surrender. Henry refused to judge them, and eventually they sought the Pope, expressing their penitence and begging for absolution. They were sentenced to pass the rest of their lives in Outremer, defending the Holy Places against the infidel; three of them went to Jerusalem, where they presently died in their beds, reconciled and absolved. But fitzUrse, the ringleader, demurred even at this light penance; he deliberately dallied on the journey, and fell sick in Calabria. There he died, and since he had not performed his penance he died excommunicate.

But King Henry had the worst death of all. In 1189 he was only fifty-six, but gluttony had made him old and sick and feeble; the Young King, his beloved heir, was already dead, and his surviving sons led all his vassals in rebellion. Young Richard hunted his father through the woods of Maine, riding unarmed and blowing a horn as though hunting a stag; when Henry saw from his window the flames of burning Le Mans, his birthplace and the city he loved best in the world, he turned his face to the wall and died, first uttering terrible imprecations which proved that he had abandoned all hope of salvation. His servants stripped the body before it was cold, and his last faithful knight, William the Marshal, had to borrow money on his private credit before he could get a coffin for it.

Yet Henry introduced important changes in the law, and since history is largely written by lawyers he has been more admired by posterity than by those who witnessed his mad rages with their own eyes. An impression has even got about that in his struggle with the Church he was victorious. He is victorious now, but victory was long delayed. For a hundred years after the Reformation clerks guilty of felony continued to plead their clergy and escape the gallows; but any felon might only plead this once, and he was branded on the thumb to show he had used his single chance. For his second felony he was hanged, and the King got his chattels. Yet this is a great improvement on the Constitutions of Clarendon, and as much as the Church obtained from any lay ruler. Thomas might well be satisfied with such a compromise.

On the much more important matter of appeals to the Papal Curia Thomas's view prevailed. Though fourteenth-century Parliaments sometimes made peevish and ineffectual complaints, appeals flowed unhindered until the Reformation. Then of course they were abolished; but a victory which lasts for 360 years is more than Waterloo or Blenheim, whose results vanished in a generation. In this fallen world no victory can be eternal.

There was something more important than legal disputes. Thomas had proved that a great King with hundreds of knights in his train might be outfaced by an unarmed man, if the unarmed man was willing to die for the Church. That tradition remains in England. Laud and the Seven Bishops in the Tower believed that the King was Supreme Governor of the Church of England, and detested Thomas of Canterbury as a Papist; but they faced Parliament and James II the more bravely because he had set the example. 'Great was he in truth always and in all places; great in the palace, great at the altar, great both at court and in the Church; great when going forth on his pilgrimage, great when returning, and singularly great at his journey's end.' So wrote Herbert of Bosham, his chaplain. His greatness endures to this day.

BIBLIOGRAPHY

I n the Rolls Series there are four volumes of contemporary lives of the saint, and three of his letters, in the original Latin. Two more volumes contain the nearly contemporary Icelandic Saga, with English translation.

W. H. Hutton: *St. Thomas Becket Archbishop of Canterbury* is a compilation in English from these sources, full of the most amusing anecdotes.

L. B. Radford: *Thomas of London before his Consecration* is a good account of his early life and of his career as Chancellor.

E. A. Abbott: *St. Thomas of Canterbury, his Death and Miracles* is a conscientious comparison of the eye-witness stories of the martyrdom, rather on the lines of Biblical Higher Criticism. The accounts kept by the monks of Canterbury of their martyr's miracles throw much light on contemporary social life and are themselves amusing.

Father John Morris: *St. Thomas of Canterbury* is written from the Papist point of view, but the facts are accurate, and he distinguishes carefully the saint's powers as Bishop, Archbishop, or Legate.

David Knowles: *The Episcopal Colleagues of Becket* is the best account of what went on in the English Church during the saint's exile. It explains the very puzzling character of Bishop Gilbert Foliot of London.

BIBLIOGRAPHY

Pollock and Maitland: *History of English Law* explains what the law courts of the middle ages were like. It is long and detailed, but one of the funniest history books ever written.

F. W. Maitland: *Roman Canon Law in the Church of England* demolishes the theory that there ever was an English Canon Law, differing from the Roman.

Doris Mary Stenton: *English Society in the Early Middle Ages* is a work of deep research, though very easy to read. I have used it extensively in the early chapters of this book.

Note

Most historians say that Thomas went to Merton as a kindergarten, and then to a London grammar school. I have inverted this order, because he must have known more than grammar before he went to Paris, and where did he learn it, except at Merton?

INDEX

Note. Henry II, King of England, Rome, and the Pope appear on almost every page of this book, and therefore are not included in the Index.

INDEX

INDEX

INDEX

226

INDEX

INDEX